SEA
SALT
AND
HONEY

SEA SALT AND HONEY

CELEBRATING THE FOOD OF KARDAMILI IN 100
SUN-DRENCHED RECIPES: A NEW GREEK COOKBOOK

**CHLOE, OLIVIA, AND NICHOLAS
TSAKIRIS**

Photographs By Romas Foord

HARPER
DESIGN

An Imprint of HarperCollinsPublishers

HarperCollins books may be purchased for educational, business, or sales promotional use. For information please email the Special Markets Department at SPsales@harpercollins.com.

First published in 2021 by Harper Design
An Imprint of HarperCollins*Publishers*
195 Broadway
New York, NY 10007 Tel: (212) 207-7000
Fax: (855) 746-6023
harperdesign@harpercollins.com www.hc.com

Distributed throughout the world by
HarperCollins*Publishers*
195 Broadway
New York, NY 10007
ISBN 978-0-06-291735-5
Library of Congress Control Number: 2020052744
Printed in Malaysia
First Printing, 2021

Interior design by Hyphenate Design
Photography by Romas Foord
Food styling by Polly Webb-Wilson
Some photographs were taken at Villa Onor, the home of Chiana Coronis and Solon Paissios:
luxuryfootprints.com

To friends and family who inspire
us always, especially David Perluck
and Craig Sax (Uncle Craig)
—Nicholas, Olivia, and Chloe

Contents

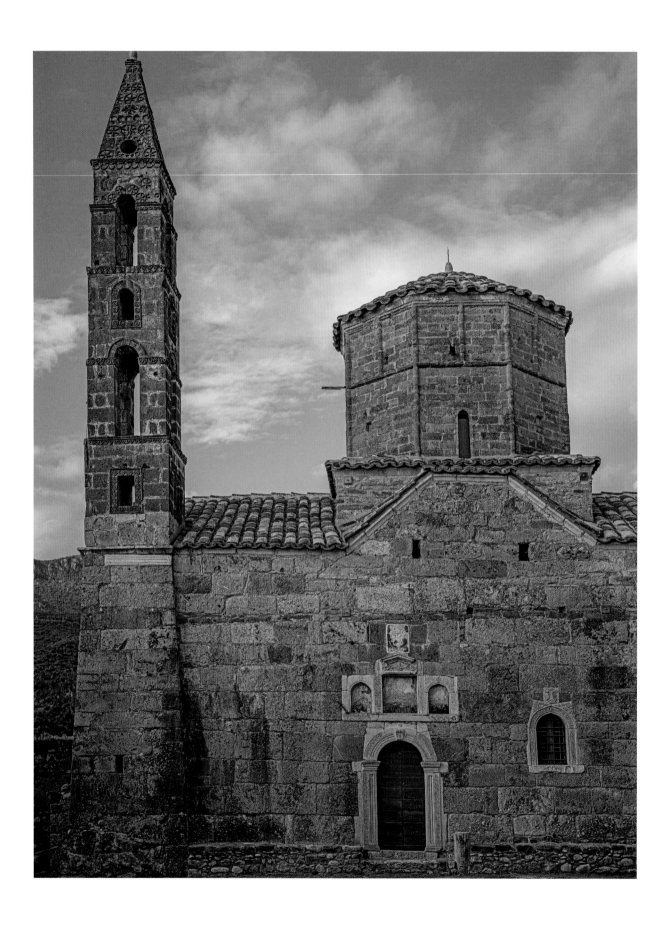

Introduction

Life in Kardamili is largely about losing track of time—and learning to be comfortable in that timelessness.

It's about using a clay pot to cook chickpeas ever so slowly, not worrying about how long it's taking to get the meal on the table, because when it's ready it'll be even more delicious for the time it took to simmer. It's about walking the twenty minutes along the beach road from home to the miniature grocery store at the edge of town, even though it would be quicker to hop in the car and drive, because the walk itself is beautiful and worth doing for its own sake. It's about harvesting sea salt, foraging in the mountains and on roadsides for wild herbs, and preserving fresh capers plucked from the salt-sprayed plants along the coast—not because it's an efficient way of doing things (though often it is—and frugal, too) but precisely *because* it takes time and requires care.

It's about savoring every aspect of life and appreciating it for what it is.

NICHOLAS

Our family has a long history in Greece, going back generations. I was born in Athens and grew up in the city and on Corfu, one of the largest islands in the Ionian Sea, on the western side of the Greek peninsula, and I spent a lot of time with family on Crete.

As a kid I loved to hang around and play in the kitchen and watch my mother and my grandmother cook. Both my grandmother and my mother were great cooks. But they had different styles. My mother leaned toward plain and simple dishes that were tasty because she knew how to use salt well. My grandmother was never afraid to experiment with herbs, spices, and unusual ingredients.

Whenever my mom cooked chicken, she always gave me the liver, which, believe it or not, was my favorite part. I loved it, but there was never enough. One day, when I was around nine—we lived on Corfu at the time—I was walking through the market and saw on a butcher's chalkboard chicken livers for two drachmas per kilo, which was something I could afford with my pocket money. I bought some. Mom was at work, so I called to ask her how she usually cooked them for me. She told me, but then she asked why. I told her that I had bought some and was going to cook them. Her reaction was surprise, quickly followed by concern that I'd burn down the kitchen. When she came home, she went straight into the kitchen to be sure all was okay. Then she grabbed a fork and tried one of my chicken livers. She said, "These are really good! You should do this more often." And that's how I started cooking.

I spent decades living out of the country—through a marriage, my daughters' child-hoods, the building of a career and a life in the United States, and a divorce. But in 2006, one of my clients opened an office in Athens, and I flew over to help with the project. As often happens in Greece, a few weeks turned into several trips of a few weeks, and the whole project took more than a year to complete. In my spare time I fled the city, with its crowded streets of building after building, the streetlights washing out the night sky, the traffic and its constant noise. I wanted to see the stars on clear nights, I wanted to feel the wind uninterrupted by office buildings, I wanted to hear the sea. On weekends I explored the Greek countryside, taking in the incred-ibly varied landscape, from beaches to sheep's meadows to mountain ranges.

The first time I visited Kardamili was on a weekend trip with friends. My relation-ship with the village wasn't a sudden whirlwind romance, but I kept visiting, even after I'd left the work in Athens and returned to the States. In Kardamili I somehow felt as if I was simultaneously on an endless vacation while also feeling at home—I loved the rugged landscape and its proud people.

Eventually, in 2007, I decided to rent a house in the village so I could come more often and my daughters could come too, on their vacations. I couldn't wait for Olivia and Chloe, who were teenagers at the time and thoroughly enjoying their lives in the United States, to join me in the village, and I was certain they'd fall under its spell as deeply as I had.

Kardamili is a village of about 450 people. From start to finish the village is a five-minute walk. The essence of life here is to be outdoors. We hike and pick herbs in the mountains, work in the garden, walk or bike the paths by the sea. The swimming season spans from April to December and we swim almost daily during that time. Cafés, restaurants, and bars are all open-air—we even celebrate New Year's Day in an outdoor restaurant. While the weather varies—some years we may be wearing sunglasses and T-shirts; other years we may be wearing scarves and sweaters—we still have our New Year's brunch outside. Since ancient times, the shelter provided by the Taygetos mountains has created a microclimate that gives us olives, figs, and all kinds of vegetables in every season.

I could never think of living in a city again. The nature of my work requires only a laptop and an internet connection. My life feels as if it has turned into a permanent vacation, even if that is far from the case. I can still work hard, but the peace here allows my mind to travel to wherever it needs to go to design, to invent, to garden, and to cook.

OLIVIA

I didn't always see the beauty of this place. When I first came to Kardamili in December 2007 from Boston, fog hung heavy over the bay, obscuring the mountains. Chloe got car sick from the winding roads. It rained the whole time, and we ended up watching DVDs in our room, dreaming of bagels and wondering why the hell Dad brought us here. But love creeps in. Dad jokes that if anyone had told him he'd end up here he'd have called them crazy. But it wasn't long before he succumbed. We all do in the end.

Many mornings, I sit in my favorite café-restaurant, Xai Xou (Hai Hou), at Melitsina Village Hotel, which is at the end of the village's white-stone beach, and look across the bay. The view never ceases to amaze me, no matter how many times I see it. With ever-changing light, it is never the same. Sipping my freddo espresso, I can look up to the powerful Taygetos mountain range jutting straight up to the sky, and below are layers of terra-cotta roofs and sand-colored stone walls that make up the town. And then there are the endlessly varying blues of the Mediterranean, hues that seem unique to Greek waters.

After making the decision to move here myself and craft a life of my own in Kardamili—near Dad and, eventually, alongside my husband, Dimitri, whose family has lived here since he was a kid, and our young son—I started to understand more clearly why we were here. The stories Dad had told Chloe and me about his own childhood and our family, while we were growing up across the Atlantic, kept coming back to me in more vivid detail. They seemed to be more than just anecdotes now—they were a part of our family and our history, connected to this place Chloe and I had at first found so unfamiliar.

Living here in such a small community, where everything I need from day to day is close by, means that I have time to just *be* with the people I care about. And I've learned to appreciate the simple things in life more than I ever dreamed I would. I don't have to work too hard to find time in the afternoon for swimming or yoga, or for a hike into the mountains. I don't have to try to figure out how to meet up with friends for dinner or drinks at a restaurant in the village. I just *do* those things. They happen organically.

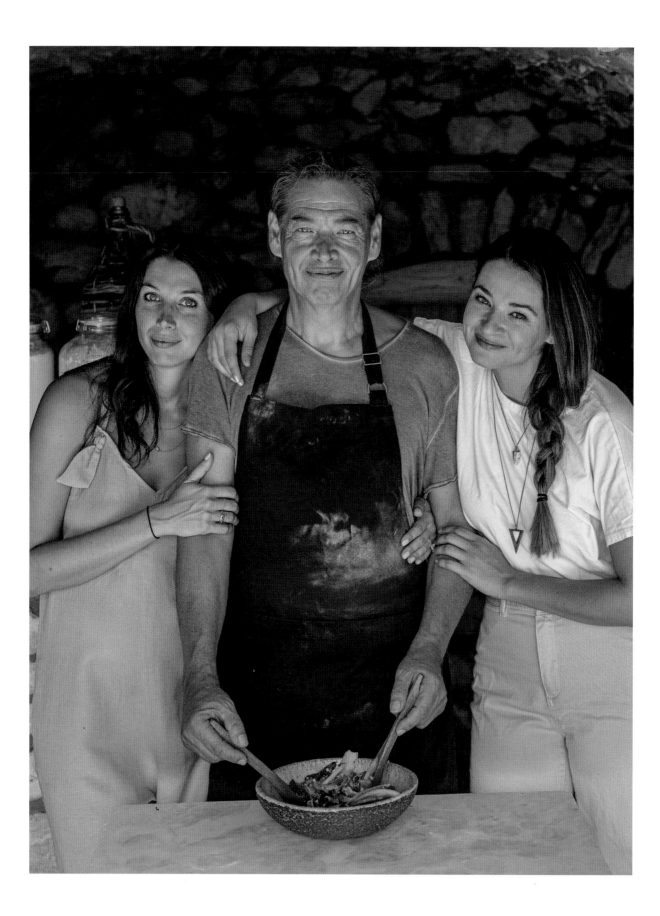

My dad's soul lies in Crete. And Cretan hospitality is known for being big-hearted and generous. From May to November, his house seems to be a weekend destination for half of Athens. He is the boss in the kitchen, with Chloe and me lending a hand as needed. His cooking style is completely improvisational, driven by what happens to be ready in the garden that day and what spices and other ingredients he feels like tinkering with that evening, as well as who is coming for dinner. And any of that can change at a moment's notice. His need to have deep conversations with each and every visitor tends to distract him from his kitchen post, and you never quite know when dinner will arrive on the table. (We always have little dishes for snacking set out, so no one truly suffers!) As much as I've tried to be helpful and jot down precise timetables and lists, there's just no way to plan for the kind of cooking he does, so we've all learned to simply take it in stride and settle in for a leisurely evening. And why not, when you're surrounded by friends, sharing stories, and having spirited debates as the night progresses, sitting at the kitchen table or out in the backyard lit by flickering candles—a glass of tsikoudia or raki in your hand that my dad is always refilling from the barrel in his kitchen.

CHLOE

Usually when people think of Greece, they imagine layered tiers of white stucco buildings with bright blue domes and matching shutters. That setting, spectacular as it is, is mostly confined to the popular tourist destination islands. The mainland is a different picture, one that is just as beautiful, just as memorable. It has a wild beauty that is unlike any other place and has as much to recommend it as any island I've seen. When I've come back here from where I live most of the year in New York, and I touch down in the Peloponnese and hear the bouzouki music once again and smell the lemon balm and sea salt in the air, I breathe again.

Time is one of the most precious gifts Kardamili offers when I'm here, which is as frequently and for as long as possible. Time to sit and talk with Livi and Dad, to appreciate the beauty of a hike up in the hills to gather herbs, to cook a meal with care, in the old style in clay pots, with produce we've grown and harvested ourselves. And to think about what I want to do with my life when I inevitably return to my apartment in New York.

I spend a lot of time at the beach when I'm in Kardamili, and it's often by myself—I think Livi and Dad are a little spoiled, living here year-round; they aren't as obsessed with being by the water all day, every day, as I am. But this is actually just fine: It gives me an opportunity to meditate, to engage in the kind of self-reflection I don't often have the time for otherwise.

When I'm not helping Dad in the kitchen I can look out to the sea from his windows. The sun here sits with my soul, and in Kardamili it is magical, the way it twinkles on the breaking waves with a friendly wink or the way it says goodnight, setting with breathtaking colors I can see through my bedroom window.

There's a freedom to our cooking, and our friends have learned to be adventurous. Its roots are firmly in the Mediterranean, but our aim is not to please the traditionalists; our culinary branches stretch to touch the Americas as well as brushing up against some northern European and Middle Eastern influences.

My dad loves to surprise our friends. Before he's taken a single bite from his plate, he'll wait and watch as our guests raise their forks and savor his latest creation. "What does it taste of?" he always asks, eagerly. Our friends never expected to find Kashmiri chiles seasoning their feta, before Dad slipped some in. Nor had they been able to single out Ethiopian berbere spice subtly altering their traditional pastitsio . . . but it was there.

Nicholas: It's already May, shall we go see if the capers are out?

Olivia: Dad, it hasn't rained for a week and it's a full moon, we should go to the Sotira path and pick sage.

Nicholas: That's a great idea. Why don't we try and get everyone together for a little party to distill it? Next week we can make soaps from the hydrosol and the essential oil. Anyway, the capers will be around for the next month and a half.

Chloe: This is not a conversation I ever thought we'd have.

Nicholas: But aren't you glad you did? *I know they're happy they did. I am too.*

This is the life we are lucky enough to lead, and we hope you'll find inspiration amid these pages—from our stories, recipes, and the captivating photography—to make some of these foods and this way of life your own. This is our family's story, the foods we cook and enjoy together, and it's all very much informed by Kardamili and what it means to live in this special place.

—NICHOLAS, OLIVIA, AND CHLOE TSAKIRIS

Our Food

Quite simply, the food we love to cook and eat is healthful, fresh, and uncomplicated. It's food that we feel good about eating every day, and also feel confident serving to guests in our home. These are dishes that reflect our local surroundings in Kardamili (and the Mediterranean in general, particularly Crete) and our lives as avid travelers and hosts. We use vegetables and herbs in season, good olive oils and healthy fats, honey instead of refined sugar, and just a little meat. To retain as many nutrients as possible, we avoid deep-frying and boiling, instead choosing to lightly sauté, simmer, poach, grill, or roast. We often slowly braise or roast dishes in clay pots called gastras, a technique that seals in flavor and nutrients.

In keeping with our way of eating well every day, some of the more traditional dishes we offer here feature adaptations we've developed to make them lighter and fresher tasting. Our version of magiritsa, a rich and creamy chowder traditionally made at Orthodox Easter with lamb offal, is vegetarian, with four different varieties of mushrooms. The pastitsio here is made with a yogurt-based béchamel rather than the usual roux-based version. Our desserts highlight fresh seasonal fruits and fine honey.

We've also included dishes that may be a little less familiar to you if all you know of Greek food is from the typical restaurant menus in the United States: dishes like briam, a meltingly tender casserole of layered vegetables in olive oil; dakos, crisp rusks we top with well-seasoned juicy summer tomatoes and peaches; and tapostalene, a made up savory cheesecake dish.

As you flip through this book, you might also notice that the selection of recipes doesn't necessarily look like that of your typical omnibus Greek cookbook. There's no hummus, no spanakopita, no moussaka. And you might be surprised to see words like *pico de gallo* and *piri piri* and *za'atar* jumping out at you from the pages.

Our food is rooted in the seasons, and we focus on making the most of the best fresh ingredients we can find that are grown and harvested near our home in Kardamili—many of them found just outside the kitchen doors, in our own gardens, and on the wild hillsides behind the village and in the sea in front of it. But we're curious eaters and cooks, and we've discovered over the years that the most delicious and interesting foods are the ones that are grounded in place while also borrowing inspiration from all over the world, using a variety of pantry ingredients—spices, chile pastes, and so on—to enhance the seasonal local produce and good-quality meats that form the foundation of our home-cooked meals.

We're travelers, and tend to become attached to new flavors we experience away from home (and we'll happily admit to feeling some nostalgia for certain foods we enjoyed when we lived together in the United States—spicy, vinegary Buffalo-wings-style sauce, for example). We'll pick up spice blends and other interesting ingredients abroad or on trips around Greece, and bring them back to our kitchens to see how they interact with the foods of home—and we always put them to good use.

A COMMUNITY OF FOOD

We don't grow and forage and raise all our own food—few people could manage such a feat, even here in the lush Outer Mani peninsula, where the growing season is long and the clay soil rich in minerals, and the mountain-protected microclimate bestows just the right amount of sun and rain. We draw on the resources of our local community of food: People who keep chickens bring their eggs to the little grocery stores in town, and we enjoy having those at hand; when we need sea salt but haven't had a chance to collect it ourselves, we can always just drop into the store and pick up a bag; there's a butcher shop in a pretty whitewashed-stone building right on the main street, perfectly convenient when we need, for example, a good cut of beef (except filet mignon— impossible to find here, to my great dismay!).

And obviously we don't cook all of our own meals: There are so many excellent restaurants, tavernas, souvlaki grills, and cafés in Kardamili and the nearby villages that we'd be foolish not to take full advantage of them. Just as Chloe does in New York, we enjoy going out to eat often, not just because the food is delicious but because we're always learning from those well-crafted meals.

I hope that some of the inspiration you take from this book is that even if you can't grow your own produce or harvest your own salt, you can help develop and support your own "community of food" wherever you live.

—OLIVIA

MULTIPLYING MY TIME

With Livi and Dad living full-time in Greece, I'm lucky to essentially have two homes—like those book authors whose bios say they "divide their time" between two cities, except I never really feel like my time is "divided." Rather, each of my homes—in New York City and Kardamili—is, in a way, amplified by the other.

I maintain a busy work and social life in New York, but my time in Kardamili has taught me the value of slowing down and savoring special moments, in particular when it comes to cooking and eating. I've been known to spend many a weekend evening on my own, carefully preparing a sweet dinner for myself inspired by meals I've enjoyed with Livi and Dad and our friends in Kardamili. And those meals, even if they stray from Livi and Dad's recipes a bit, often feature some of the souvenirs I've brought back from Greece: I don't shop for shoes or clothes or handbags when I travel; I shop for olive oil and cheese knives (and I'd be perfectly happy to ditch several outfits' worth of clothes to make room for foods and cooking supplies in my luggage).

Similarly, my life in New York has informed how I interact with the precious time I get to spend in Kardamili. It's not that I *rush* to do everything I possibly can in the time I have in Greece, but I do make a point of not taking anything for granted. I make sure I'm able to spend whole days at the beach or hiking in the mountains, and hours in the kitchen and at the table with my family—and I never lose sight of the fact that the memories of these experiences are what will sustain me when I head back to my life in the city.

—CHLOE

So here you'll find tuna salad featuring not just the capers that grow all around our village but also za'atar, an herby spice blend common on the other side of the Mediterranean, in the Middle East. You'll see fiery salsas inspired by the Mexican foods we love in the States, but with a decidedly Greek character. And you shouldn't be surprised to find dishes using North African harissa or Ethiopian berbere, which, it turns out, complement even our more traditional foods extremely well.

CHLOE

Living in New York City, I'm kind of obsessed with keeping on top of all the trendy new foods that pop up on my radar. I'm always telling Livi and Dad about dishes they should try to re-create, and of course I do plenty of experimenting myself in my apartment's mini-kitchen—often based on a foundation of Greek ingredients and techniques. A lot of those multicultural references have made their way into the recipes in this book.

NICHOLAS

These recipes are meant to be made your own. Chloe, Livi, and I adapt and experiment and improvise every time we step into the kitchen with an idea, however vague, of what we'd like to cook, and I'd encourage you to use these recipes as jumping-off points that will inspire your own creativity.

If you feel like our zucchini, cured ham, and sage pasta would be delicious tonight but don't have zucchini, use some lovely asparagus from the farmers' market instead. Try drizzling the Sea Salt and Honey Hot Sauce #3 (page 67) on roasted carrots or crisped chickpeas instead of cauliflower. If your fishmonger doesn't have fresh cod today, ask her to recommend a different fish that would work well in our baked cod dish.

Taste as you go, as we do, adding a little more salt or spice, herbs or lemon juice, for example, until it appeals to you and is right for the people you're serving—don't be too concerned about sticking exactly to the quantities in each recipe. If the seasoning tastes right to you, it's right.

In short, be flexible, take your time in the kitchen (but, as Livi and Chloe would beg me, not *too much* time), enjoy your meals with good friends and family, and it'll all be delicious.

Our Kitchen Tools and Ingredients

NICHOLAS

In my kitchen, large bunches of wild and homegrown herbs hang from a steel rod above the countertop, and shelves of clear glass jars of staple ingredients—unlabeled, because it's not as if we'd forget what dried lentils or chickpeas look like—line the walls. There's a big steel container of olive oil that we tap to fill smaller clear glass bottles that stand ready to use for sautéing or drizzling over vegetables and salads. Spices in clear glass jars are stashed . . . well, everywhere: A fair amount of counter space and multiple cupboards are devoted to my always-expanding collection, in addition to a large basket (or two or three) in other areas of the house.

Other essentials in our kitchens are gastras, the glazed and unglazed clay pots for long, slow cooking in the oven (see page 177; our gastras are from the island of Sifnos, which is known for its pottery because of its good clay). We also recommend having a solid mortar and pestle on hand for crushing spices and grinding fresh chiles into pastes, and sturdy wooden cutting boards: one for produce, one for meats, and one for bread.

Following are some of the common and more specialized ingredients you'll find used throughout the book.

Olive oil: We love butter, but use it only rarely, so you won't find any in this book—we use olive oil almost exclusively. It's the most healthful of cooking and dressing oils, high in monounsaturated fats for a healthy heart—for some people it also aids digestion. Our family goes through 25 to 30 kilograms (55 to 66 pounds) of olive oil a year, but since we don't do a lot of deep-frying (and there's none in these recipes) we feel comfortable using the best-quality extra-virgin olive oils we can obtain. We make our own oil and we also buy oil from an outfit that processes olives from small groves around Kardamili—nearly every family has olive trees in their yards, to preserve and eat and to bring to the processor to crush and spin. The Bläuel company, which makes Mani brand olive oil and has a quaint shop on the main street in town, is committed to sustainable practices and sells oils made to the highest standards and only from organic fruit.

Seasonal vegetables and fruits: We grow as much of our own produce as possible, without pesticides or commercial fertilizers, and head to the hills to gather weeds like nettles, dandelion, purslane, and amaranth (known collectively as horta). If you don't have room for a garden, just buy the best you can, preferably organic and from a trusted source.

Capers: We harvest caper berries from the trailing bushes that grow in the coastal crevices along the gulf (see page 91) and preserve them ourselves. Look for good-quality Greek capers preserved in brine.

Mushrooms: Fresh portobello, cremini, white button, and oyster mushrooms are all readily available in our local grocery stores, and we use them extensively. I often pick up dried mushrooms on trips around Greece—on a recent trip to Kilkis, in the north, I bought two kilos (otherwise known as "a lot") of dried shiitakes and several kinds of wild mountain mushrooms I don't know the names of.

Dried pulses: We always have chickpeas, brown lentils, fava (yellow split peas—not to be confused with fava beans or broad beans), and a variety of other dried beans on hand in tightly sealed jars. Many of the pulses we use are from Epirus and Santorini—a lot are grown in Thessaly, but we avoid those: too many pesticides. The Greek chickpeas we use are a slightly smaller variety than is common in the United States, but any kind will do.

Yogurt: There's something about the yogurt here that's apparently hard to replicate elsewhere: It's thick, of course, but also fluffy on the palate, almost like whipped cream, and it's often not quite as tart as yogurts available in the States. That said, Fage brand is a good choice for use in any of our recipes.

Cheeses: Feta and goat cheese, as well as fresh mizithra (a soft sheep's or goat's milk cheese similar to a strained ricotta), are featured prominently on our table and in these recipes. Mizithra can be hard to find outside Greece, but we've suggested substitutions that will work well in each recipe.

Seafood: The species that are common here may not always be available in your markets, but we've tailored these recipes to work well with a wide range of fish and seafood. Don't hesitate to ask your fishmonger for advice on substitutions.

Good-quality meats in small quantities: We're not vegetarians, but we generally reserve meat for special occasions or once- or twice-weekly meals, or for when we go out to eat (a souvlaki restaurant at the north end of town is a favorite). Greek home cooks make an effort to use as much of the animal as possible, and in our family dishes featuring chicken liver and beef liver are highly anticipated.

Siglino: Siglino is a smoked pork product found throughout the Mani and Crete. Smoked with wild sage branches and preserved in pork fat, it's served both heated and cold. It's worth seeking out online; you can substitute very good-quality smoked ham, but the flavor won't be quite as intense.

Spices and dried herbs: Berbere, za'atar, curry powder, piri piri, and dry harissa are favorite spice blends in our kitchen. You can make them as you go, or mix up a good-size batch of each (see page 35) and keep them in tightly sealed containers for up to several months. Kashmiri chiles, dried Greek oregano, marjoram, sage, and thyme also come up often in our recipes.

Bay leaves: We always use whole (not broken) dried bay leaves and remove them when the food is cooked. The reason is to avoid small pieces breaking off and remaining in the food. Bay leaves are very hard and have very sharp edges, which could cut you internally if swallowed, so it is imperative that they are totally removed.

Sea salt: For our savory dishes, we use flaky, unprocessed sea salt gathered from the beach at Kardamili (see page 91), and it has a very distinctive texture and flavor. Unless noted in the recipe, all our measurements are for flaky salt, but you can use fine table salt instead, adjusting the quantities: If a recipe calls for 3 teaspoons flaky salt, use 2 teaspoons fine table salt. And, as always, taste often and season to your liking.

Honey: The wildflowers blanketing the mountains here make honey from the Mani some of the most treasured in Greece. We use it liberally to replace refined sugar—honey has medicinal qualities and also just tastes better in our foods. Sweet mountain honey works well with meats like chicken and pork and in desserts. "Bitter" honey, produced from the evergreen strawberry tree (*Arbutus unedo*) or wild heather, is an acquired taste but is wonderful in vinaigrettes. Taste the different honeys available at your farmers' markets or good grocers and pick a local variety you like.

Flours: In our kitchen we use organic flours—rye, whole wheat, and farro (*zea* in Greek), an ancient variety of wheat that has a high protein content and is lower in gluten than regular wheat—as well as all-purpose.

MONASTERY HERBS

In spring and summer we drive half an hour up into the mountains behind Kardamili, on a twisty road that passes through the ruins of an ancient quarry and the picturesque villages of Proastio and Exochori, the side of the road dotted with miniature churches no bigger than toolsheds, each marking the violent death of someone or other during the era of vendettas and feuds. We pass, too, the remains of one of the famous eighteenth-century stone tower houses, this one named for the Kitriniaris family. When we reach a high valley at the edge of a designated wilderness area, we pull over and start to walk, big reusable grocery totes and clippers in hand.

We head toward the Vaidenitsa monastery ruins a little ways up the valley. All along the path are wild herbs, and we snip and bag, snip and bag, on our way up—always being sure to take just a few sprigs from each plant. This is goat territory, and the climb is steep in spots, but shady and breezy, and we know that just past the ruins there's a freshwater spring, marked with a painted wooden arrow, where we can fill our stainless-steel camp mugs with ice-cold water.

Depending on the time of year, we might find any of the following:

Asfaka: False sage or Jerusalem sage (*Phlomis fruticosa*)—the leaves look like sage's, but it has large clusters of yellow flowers. It's good for medicinal teas, but isn't a substitute for sage.

Bay laurel: A huge bay tree (*Laurus nobilis*) overhangs a lovely pool of water in the stream that runs down the valley past the ruins of the monastery and the (more recent-vintage) water mill, and younger shrubs can be found sprouting up throughout the surrounding woods.

Melissa: Here we have a wild herb the locals call simply melissa; it's in the same family as common lemon balm (*Melissa officinalis*). It's a main ingredient in our Cleanse and Soothe Tea Blend (page 262).

Sage: We pick long branches of wild sage (*Salvia fruticosa*) when it's in full flower and the leaves' essential oils are at peak and hang them in bundles to dry.

St. John's wort: In the shops in Kardamili you can find small bottles of bright red olive oil infused with St. John's wort (*Hypericum perforatum*), which is used topically to treat burns, scrapes, and cuts.

Thyme: Native thyme (*Thymus vulgaris*) grows like mad on roadsides and up into the hills, and we collect large sprigs of it for drying at home.

And the strange ferny thing that grows in and near the stream and is possibly used in Japanese cuisine: There's clearly a lot we're still learning about the Mani's native flora.

Spice Blends

Here are four of our favorite go-to spice blends. Add one of these to just about anything to get a brand-new version of your favorite recipe.

BERBERE
4 teaspoons ground fenugreek
1 teaspoon ground nigella
2 teaspoons ground kings cumin
    (ajowan)
1 teaspoon ground black
    cardamom
3 teaspoons paprika
1 teaspoon garlic powder
3 teaspoons ground cayenne
    pepper
1 teaspoon sea salt flakes

PIRI-PIRI
1 teaspoon ground long pepper
1 teaspoon rose petal flakes
1 teaspoon dried oregano
1 teaspoon dried thyme
1 teaspoon lemon zest
1 teaspoon chile flakes
1 teaspoon dried basil
½ teaspoon sea salt flakes

HARISSA
1½ teaspoons paprika
1 teaspoon ground ginger
1 teaspoon dried oregano
1 teaspoon ground cardamom
1 teaspoon garlic powder
1 teaspoon onion powder
1 teaspoon ground cayenne pepper
½ teaspoon sea salt flakes

ZA'ATAR
1 teaspoon dried oregano
2 teaspoons dried thyme
2 teaspoons sumac
2 teaspoons sesame seeds
½ teaspoon sea salt flakes

1. For each spice mix, in a small bowl, combine all the ingredients.
2. Whisk the spices together until evenly combined.
3. Stored in an airtight glass jar, these spice blends can keep for a year. Never store spice mixes in plastic.

CHAPTER ONE

To Share at the Table

Mezes and Snacks, Sauces and Salsas

Φάγαμε μαζί ψωμί και αλάτι.

We ate bread and salt together.

traditional dakos

Serves 2 to 4

Barley rusks (1 large or 4 small),
    store-bought or homemade
    (page 235)
¼ cup (60 ml) extra-virgin olive oil
3 large fresh tomatoes
Sea salt flakes and freshly ground
    black pepper
1 cup (245 g) crumbled fresh
    mizithra (see Note) or feta
¼ cup (30 g) capers, drained
    brined or rinsed salted
1 tablespoon fresh thyme

This beautifully simple Cretan dish is a staple on the meze table and for breakfast. The nutritious, coarse-textured barley rusks soften a little under generous drizzles of olive oil and juicy grated tomatoes, but still retain some crispness.

1. If your rusks are extremely hard, soften them by sprinkling them with 2 to 4 tablespoons water.
2. Drizzle a bit of olive oil over the rusks.
3. Cut the tomatoes in half, grate them, and spread the grated flesh on top of the rusks.
4. Add sea salt flakes and freshly ground black pepper to taste.
5. Sprinkle the cheese on top, and top that with the capers and thyme.
6. Drizzle with some more oil and serve.

NOTE: Mizithra is a mild-flavored cheese made with goat's or sheep's milk. The fresh version, which you should use here, is somewhat similar to a thick ricotta, while aged mizithra is hard and grate-able.

peach and goat cheese dakos with basil and balsamic drizzle

Serves 2 to 4

1 cup (240 ml) balsamic vinegar
¼ cup (60 ml) honey
Barley rusks (1 large or 4 small), store-bought or homemade (page 235)
4 peaches
1 cup (115 g) crumbled goat cheese
¼ cup (13 g) chopped fresh mint
¼ cup (10 g) chopped fresh basil
¼ cup (60 ml) extra-virgin olive oil

Peach dakos could be served as an appetizer to share with friends or consumed on your own as a refreshing lunch by the sea.

1. To make the balsamic drizzle, in a small saucepan over medium-high heat, combine the vinegar and honey and bring to a boil. Lower the heat and continue to simmer until the mixture has reduced to about ⅓ cup (80 ml), about 10 minutes. Remove from the heat and let cool.
2. Meanwhile, moisten the rusks with 2 to 4 tablespoons water to soften them.
3. Pit the peaches, grate them, and spread the grated flesh on top of the rusks.
4. Sprinkle the cheese over the peaches.
5. Top with the mint and basil.
6. Drizzle generously with the olive oil and the balsamic drizzle. Serve.

spicy and crisp oven-baked piri-piri fries

Serves 4 to 6

3 to 4 thin-skinned potatoes,
    such as Yukon gold
¼ cup (60 ml) extra-virgin olive oil
1 to 2 teaspoons piri-piri spice
    blend (page 35)
1 teaspoon sea salt flakes

Piri-piri means "pepper pepper" or "hot pepper" and refers to a specific variety of hot chile used throughout Africa. It's also used to refer to a spice blend and a Portuguese sauce made with the chiles, which are similar to pequin chiles and are often a bit hotter than cayenne. We use an herb-heavy spice blend featuring ground long pepper, which was the pepper used in original versions of piri-piri.

1. Wash and scrub the potatoes; if they aren't organic, peel them.

2. Use a fry cutter or a knife to cut the potatoes into ¼- to ⅝-inch- (6- to 16-mm-) wide strips as consistently as possible for even baking.

3. In a bowl, cover the potatoes with cold water (enough water to cover them twice), stir with your hand, drain, and repeat two more times. In the third bath, leave the potatoes to soak for 30 minutes. This process, done to remove some of the starch, is the secret to making them crispy.

4. Preheat the oven to 425°F (220°C). Line a large baking sheet with parchment paper.

5. Drain the potatoes well and pat them with paper towels or dry them in a salad spinner.

6. In a bowl, toss the potatoes with the olive oil and piri-piri. Spread the potatoes in a single layer on the prepared baking sheet, making sure they do not touch one another. Sprinkle the salt evenly on top. Bake for 15 to 20 minutes, flip the fries over, lower the oven temperature to 350°F (175°C), and bake for another 15 to 20 minutes, until crisp and browned. Serve and enjoy.

potato croquettes with kefalotiri, parsley, and dill

Serves 8 to 10

2½ pounds (1.2 kg) thin-skinned potatoes, such as Yukon gold

2 cups (230 g) grated kefalotiri cheese (you can substitute pecorino or Romano)

4 large eggs, separated

¼ cup (50 g) grated onion (or minced in a food processor)

¼ cup (9 g) minced fresh parsley

¼ cup (13 g) minced fresh dill

1½ teaspoons sea salt flakes

1½ teaspoons freshly ground black pepper

2 to 3 cups (300 g) dry bread crumbs, plus more as needed (see Note)

Extra-virgin olive oil for brushing

Traditionally, croquettes are fried in olive oil, but baking them, as we do here, works just as well.

1. In a pot of water to cover, boil the potatoes with their peels over high heat just until fork tender but not falling apart, about 30 minutes.

2. Preheat the oven to 400°F (205°C). Line a baking sheet with parchment paper.

3. Drain the potatoes and let them cool enough so you can handle them. Peel and mash them in a bowl. Add the cheese, egg yolks, onion, parsley, dill, salt, and pepper. Mix well.

4. Make soup spoon–size balls of the potato mixture, then flatten them a little bit.

5. In a bowl, beat the egg whites, just to break up the whites. Place the bread crumbs in a separate shallow bowl. One at a time, coat the potato discs in bread crumbs, then dip in the egg whites, then coat in bread crumbs again. Place on the prepared baking sheet and brush the tops with olive oil.

6. Bake for 20 minutes, or until golden brown. Serve hot.

NOTE: Fresh and panko crumbs work too.

buttermilk cauliflower tossed in buffalo sauce

Serves 2 to 4

1 cup (240 ml) buttermilk

½ cup (65 g) all-purpose flour

1 teaspoon sea salt flakes

1 teaspoon pressed garlic

1 small head cauliflower, separated
   into small florets (about
   2½ cups/335 g)

½ cup (120 ml) Sea Salt and Honey
   Hot Sauce #3 (page 67)

Gorgonzola Greek Yogurt Dip
   (page 68)

Occasionally, I get a serious craving for the dishes I used to love back home in the States—and one in particular: buffalo wings. Named after the city in western New York State, rather than the animal, they're chicken wings that are deep-fat fried, tossed in a buttery hot sauce, and served with a blue-cheese dip. But one year, when Dad and I had grown plentiful cauliflowers, we came up with our own vegetarian version. We bake the cauliflower florets instead of frying them, toss them in a homemade hot sauce, and serve with a creamy gorgonzola dip. They make for ideal meze or a sunshine snack accompanied by a cold beer.

—OLIVIA

1. Preheat the oven to 450°F (230°C). Line a baking sheet with parchment paper.

2. Start by making the buttermilk marinade: In a bowl, mix the buttermilk, flour, salt, and garlic.

3. Add the cauliflower to the marinade, toss to coat, and let stand for 15 minutes.

4. Arrange the florets on the prepared baking sheet, making sure they do not touch one another. Bake for 15 to 20 minutes, until they are nicely golden in color.

5. In a bowl, toss the florets with the hot sauce. Serve with the dip.

TIP: To make a simple buttermilk-yogurt dip, mix another batch of the buttermilk marinade, replacing the flour with 1 cup (240 ml) whole milk Greek yogurt.

crunchy okra

Serves 4

1 pound (455 g) fresh and tender
   okra
½ cup (70 g) yellow cornmeal
½ teaspoon sea salt flakes
¼ teaspoon freshly ground black
   pepper
4 tablespoons extra-virgin olive oil
1 teaspoon cumin seeds (optional)

You don't need a ton of oil to fry okra—just use a slick of olive oil in a skillet and turn the okra slices gently as they brown. This makes a great starter, something to snack on with drinks before dinner.

1. Rinse the okra well and put in a colander to drain. Pat with a towel to completely dry. Slice the okra pods crosswise into ¼-inch (6-mm) pieces.

2. In a large bowl, mix together the cornmeal, salt, and pepper. Toss the okra pieces in the mixture to coat well.

3. Heat the olive oil in a cast-iron skillet over high heat. Using a slotted spoon, carefully add the okra. Toss in the cumin seeds (if using). Cook over medium heat for 2 to 3 minutes until golden brown, then turn with a spatula. Continue to cook the other side for 2 to 3 minutes until golden brown.

4. Remove the okra from the pan with the slotted spoon, place on a paper towel to remove any excess oil, and serve.

zucchini chips

Serves 2

2 small zucchini
¼ cup (60 ml) extra-virgin olive oil
½ teaspoon sea salt flakes
½ teaspoon freshly ground black
    pepper
Dried oregano

For a spicier version, we like to sprinkle our harissa or piri-piri spice blend (page 35) on top before baking.

1. Preheat the oven to 425°F (220°C). Line a baking sheet with parchment paper.

2. Slice the zucchini into circles, as thin as possible, no more than ⅛ inch (3 mm) thick, ideally with a mandoline.

3. Put the zucchini in a large bowl. Add the olive oil, salt, and pepper. Toss until all the slices are evenly coated.

4. Arrange the zucchini in a single layer on the prepared baking sheet. Bake for 20 to 25 minutes, until golden and crispy, tossing halfway through.

5. Sprinkle oregano on top and serve.

OREGANO

Everyone knows that Greeks love their oregano, but unless you've spent at least a couple weeks here you might not realize the extent to which this herb is venerated. In the small grocery stores in Kardamili, bunches of dried oregano the size of Mother's Day bouquets are propped in baskets by the door, and it's used with a much more generous hand than is generally the case in the States, especially on souvlaki.

My husband, Dimitri, told us how his mother, unbeknownst to him, packed a giant bag of pungent oregano in his suitcase when he left Greece to go off to university—because clearly he would *need more oregano* where he was headed. The luggage sailed through various security checkpoints, but when Dimitri opened it up on arrival, he found that the bag of dried herb had burst and every item of clothing he'd brought with him had been seasoned like a plate of kebabs.

—OLIVIA

nettle and spinach pie

Serves 6 to 8

FOR THE PHYLLO

4 cups (375 g) all-purpose flour,
plus more for dusting
½ teaspoon sea salt flakes
½ cup (120 ml) extra-virgin olive
oil, plus more for brushing

FOR THE FILLING

1 pound (455 g) nettles
1 pound (455 g) spinach
¼ cup (60 ml) olive oil
2 teaspoons freshly ground black
pepper
1 large onion, finely chopped
1 teaspoon sea salt flakes
6 to 8 scallions, chopped (white
part ⅛ inch/3 mm thick; green
part ½ to ¾ inch/12 to 20 mm)
1 cup (150 g) crumbled feta cheese
½ cup (25 g) fresh mint, chopped
1 cup (50 g) fresh parsley, chopped
1 cup (50 g) fennel fronds or fresh
dill, chopped
2 large eggs, beaten

TO PUT IT ALL TOGETHER

Extra-virgin olive oil
2 tablespoons fine semolina
More flour for dusting
2 tablespoons sesame seeds

For this dish we like to make our phyllo dough from scratch, because the pie benefits from a phyllo that's a little thicker than the standard frozen grocery-store variety. If you don't have nettles, you can omit them and double the quantity of spinach (and vice versa if you have lots of nettles and no spinach on hand).

1. Make the phyllo: In a chilled bowl, combine the flour and salt. Add the olive oil and mix with a spoon.

2. Add 1½ cups (360 ml) water and knead to a soft, smooth dough that does not stick to the sides. If it is sticky, add 1 tablespoon flour at a time and keep kneading until it does not stick anymore. If it is crumbly, add 1 tablespoon water at a time and keep kneading until it is all smooth. Divide the dough into two balls.

3. Flour the work surface where you are going to roll out your dough and, using a floured rolling pin, roll out one ball at a time. As you are rolling you can sprinkle a little bit of flour to make rolling easier and to keep the phyllo from shrinking. Roll the dough out till it is about ¹⁄₁₆ inch (2 mm) thick and 11 to 12 inches (28 to 30 cm) in length and width.

4. Brush the entire surface with olive oil and fold two opposite sides to meet in the center and brush the surfaces that were folded with olive oil. Repeat with the other two sides to meet in the center. Fold in half, brush with oil, and fold in half again.

5. Brush olive oil on both sides of the dough, wrap in plastic wrap, and put it in the refrigerator to chill and rest for at least 45 minutes and up to 2 days. Repeat with the second dough ball.

6. Make the filling: Wearing gloves, wash the nettles and spinach and keep them separate. From the nettles, keep only the leaves and the tender stems from the top. Set aside in a colander to drain.

7. Heat the olive oil in a large deep saucepan over high heat. Add the pepper and lower the heat to medium-high. Add the onion, sprinkle 1 teaspoon salt over it, and let cook undisturbed for 30 seconds. Stir well and cook until translucent, 2 to 5 minutes.

8. Add the spinach and cook until it is all wilted, a few minutes, then add the nettles and the scallions. As soon as the nettles are wilted, remove the pan from the heat and mix in the cheese and herbs.

9. At this point you want to drain any liquid from the pan. If there is a lot, drain it in a colander for a few minutes, then put the mixture back in the pan. Add the eggs and mix well.

10. Put it all together: Preheat the oven to 325°F (165°C).

11. Brush the bottom of a 9-inch (23-cm) pie dish with olive oil and sprinkle the semolina over it.

12. Flour your work surface and rolling pin. Unwrap but don't unfold one of the phyllo packages from the fridge and roll it out to a circle large enough to overhang the pie dish by 1 to 1½ inches (2.5 to 4 cm).

13. Lay the phyllo in the dish and let the sides overhang the rim. Brush oil over the entire surface. Pour in the nettle mixture and spread it out evenly.

14. Take the other phyllo package from the fridge and roll it out, this time only ¼ to ½ inch (6 to 12 mm) bigger than the pie dish. (It will be a little thicker than the bottom layer.) Lay it on top of the filling. Roll the edges of the bottom phyllo and top phyllo up and together toward the middle to form a ½-inch (12-mm) rim all around. With a sharp knife, cut five or six slits about 2 inches (5 cm) long in the top crust. Brush the entire surface with oil and sprinkle with the sesame seeds.

15. Bake for 50 to 60 minutes, until the phyllo is golden brown. Cut and serve warm or at room temperature.

A HOT PAN, OLIVE OIL, AND BLACK PEPPER

You'll notice that at the beginning of many of our recipes, we have you heat the olive oil in a pan over high heat, then add black pepper, immediately turning the heat down and adding more ingredients (garlic, onion, and so on). We almost never grind pepper over a dish at the end, as other cooks might, because cooking the spice ever so briefly in hot oil helps bring out its own essential oils, which means it imparts more flavor to the food.

But here's a secret: This method—heat olive oil in the pan, then add the pepper—isn't really how we do it. We've worded it this way in the recipes because we feel that's the "safest" option for readers who might not be used to working with oil and pepper this way. What we usually do, in fact, is heat the pepper in the pan until it starts to smoke, then immediately (immediately is very important because if the pepper really smokes and you breathe in the fumes you will start coughing to no end) add the olive oil and let it cook until it's fragrant but not burned, and only then start adding more ingredients. When you feel confident that you'll be able to identify the point where the pepper is *just starting* to smoke, go for it! You'll be cooking exactly as we do here in Kardamili.

tapostalene—savory mini cheesecakes

Serves 8

¼ cup (60 ml) extra-virgin olive oil, plus more for brushing
3 sheets phyllo dough, cut into 4- to 6-inch (10- to 15-cm) squares (depending on the size of your ramekins)
½ teaspoon freshly ground black pepper, plus more if needed
8 button mushrooms, sliced
2 leeks, sliced and rinsed well
1 teaspoon sea salt flakes
8 broccoli florets, sliced
2 large eggs
1 cup (150 g) crumbled feta cheese
¾ cup (180 g) crumbled fresh mizithra cheese (or manouri or ricotta)
1 cup (240 ml) whole milk Greek yogurt
1 cup (240 ml) heavy cream or milk

This recipe is something that came to my head and, not knowing what to call them, I named them "tapostalene," which in Greek is four words, Τα πως τα λενε, meaning something like "Whatchamacallit."

—NICHOLAS

1. Preheat the oven to 350°F (175°C).

2. Brush the insides of 8 small ramekins with olive oil and line with phyllo squares: one layer if the phyllo is thick, two or three if it is thin (brushing a little oil between layers). Place on a baking sheet.

3. Bake for 6 minutes. Take out and set aside. Leave the oven on.

4. In a large saucepan, heat ¼ cup (60 ml) of the olive oil over high heat, then add the pepper and lower the heat to medium-high. Add the mushrooms and cook, stirring with a wooden spoon, for 3 to 4 minutes, then add the leeks and salt and cook for 3 minutes more. Add the broccoli and cook for an additional 2 minutes, then remove from the heat and set aside.

5. In a large bowl, combine the eggs, feta, mizithra, yogurt, and cream, and mix all together using an immersion blender until the mixture is homogenized.

6. To each baked phyllo cup add 1 tablespoon of the egg mixture and 2 to 3 tablespoons of the vegetable mixture. Top up each cup with more of the egg mixture.

7. Place in the oven and bake for 20 to 25 minutes, until the tops start to rise and become golden. The tops will settle after you take them out of the oven, and that is normal. Let them cool. Serve warm, at room temperature, or cold.

baked beef keftedes

Serves 4

4 or 5 slices stale bread, crusts
    removed
1 cup (240 ml) milk
1 shot (1½ ounces/45 ml) ouzo
1 cup (125 g) finely minced onions
1½ teaspoons minced garlic
⅔ cup (35 g) minced fresh parsley
5 tablespoons (11 g) dried mint,
    or 2 cups (50 g) minced
    fresh mint
2 large eggs
1 pound (455 g) ground beef
2 teaspoons sea salt flakes
1 teaspoon freshly ground black
    pepper
3 tablespoons extra-virgin olive
    oil, plus more for coating the
    meatballs

Keftedes—fried meatballs—are a staple in Greece. When a friend opened a bar in Kardamili, he asked Dad his advice on making the perfect keftedes—but the catch was that he didn't want them fried. So we began playing around, trying to find a healthier way to cook them, without compromising on taste or texture. We tried several methods of baking them, experimenting with ways to keep them crispy on the outside and moist on the inside. The first two attempts were unsuccessful, but our third attempt, in which we brushed the meatballs with olive oil halfway through baking, was a real winner in look, feel, and taste. They are now a popular item on the bar menu.
—OLIVIA

1. Preheat the oven to 400°F (205°C). Line a baking sheet with parchment paper.

2. Cut the bread into ½- to ¾-inch (12- to 19-mm) cubes. In a large bowl, soak the crumbs in the milk and ouzo while you prepare the rest of the ingredients. Using sliced bread instead of bread crumbs makes the meatballs fluffier.

3. In a bowl, combine the onions, garlic, parsley, and mint.

4. To the bread mixture, add the onion mixture along with the eggs, beef, salt, pepper, and the 3 tablespoons olive oil. Mix well with your hands and then let sit for 20 to 30 minutes.

5. Take a spoonful of the meat mixture and roll it into a ball about the size of a golf ball with your hands. Place on the prepared baking sheet. Repeat with the remaining meat mixture.

6. Bake the meatballs for 15 minutes. Remove the baking sheet from the oven and brush the meatballs with olive oil, then turn them over and brush the other sides with olive oil. Bake for another 10 to 12 minutes, until cooked through. Serve hot.

spicy berbere chicken pies

Makes 20 to 24 pies

¼ cup (60 ml) extra-virgin olive oil,
 plus more for brushing
½ teaspoon freshly ground black
 pepper, plus more if needed
1 pound (455 g) boneless, skinless
 chicken thighs, chopped
2 cloves garlic, minced
1½ cups (85 g) chopped scallions
 (white parts ⅛ inch/3 mm
 thick, green parts ½ to
 ¾ inch/12 to 20 mm)
2 portobello mushroom caps,
 chopped (about 3½ cups/
 300 g)
2 teaspoons sea salt flakes
2 teaspoons berbere spice blend
 (page 35)
½ pound (225 g) potatoes,
 preferably Yukon gold, boiled,
 peeled, and mashed with a
 fork
1½ cups (60 g) chopped fresh
 cilantro
3 tablespoons sesame seeds
5 to 6 sheets phyllo dough

These little phyllo pastries, with an intensely spiced chicken and mushroom filling, are perfect for the meze table or as a light lunch with a green salad.

1. In a large saucepan, heat the olive oil over high heat, then add the black pepper and turn the heat down to medium-high. Add the chicken and cook, stirring with a wooden spoon, until browned on all sides. Stir in the garlic and cook until fragrant, about 2 minutes.

2. Add the scallions and mushrooms and sprinkle the salt over them, then let cook undisturbed for 30 seconds. Add the berbere. Mix well and continue to stir for 1 minute or so, then lower the heat to medium and cook for 6 minutes more.

3. Remove from the heat, add the mashed potatoes and cilantro, and mix very well.

4. Preheat the oven to 350°F (175°C). Sprinkle about half of the sesame seeds evenly on a baking sheet.

5. Cut each phyllo sheet into four strips.

6. Centered at the end of a strip and about one inch from the end, place 1 tablespoon of the filling; it should cover about half of the width of the strip. Fold the bottom up over the filling and fold again, then brush the top with a light coat of olive oil. Fold both long sides of the phyllo strip so they meet in the center, brush with olive oil, and fold the filling up in the rest of the strip.

7. Repeat until all the filling is gone or all the phyllo is gone.

8. Brush a bit of olive oil on both sides of each phyllo package, set them on the baking sheet on top of the sesame seeds, then sprinkle with more sesame seeds.

9. Bake for 20 to 25 minutes, until golden brown. These are best served hot, but they're also delicious cold.

rooster's beak mediterranée— a fresh and fiery summer salsa

Serves 4 to 6

3 tomatoes, cut into ¼- to ½-inch
(6- to 12-mm) cubes (about
3 cups/540 g)
1 onion, preferably white, finely
diced (about ¾ cup/95 g)
2 fresh or dried serrano, jalapeño,
or habanero chiles, finely
diced
½ cup (20 g) finely chopped fresh
cilantro
2 teaspoons ground cumin
Juice of 1 lime
2 teaspoons sea salt flakes, or to
taste

Serve this spicy fresh salsa (photograph follows), inspired by the Mexican pico de gallo ("rooster's beak"—the origin of the colorful name is up for debate), with corn tortilla chips or crackers.

1. In a bowl, combine the tomatoes, onion, chiles, cilantro, cumin, and lime juice. Toss to mix and add salt to taste. Let stand for 15 to 20 minutes, then toss once more and serve.

orange pico de gallo—a winter salsa fresca

Serves 6 to 8

3 oranges, peeled, seeded, and cut into ¼- to ½-inch (6- to 12-mm) pieces (about 3 cups/540 g)

1 onion, preferably white, finely diced (about ¾ cup/95 g)

2 dried serrano, jalapeño, or habanero chiles, finely diced

½ cup (20 g) finely chopped fresh cilantro

2 teaspoons ground cumin

Juice of 1 lime

2 teaspoons sea salt flakes, or to taste

Since tomatoes and chiles are not in season in the winter, we use oranges and dried chiles to make a very twisted—but delicious—pico de gallo. And why not? Oranges are acidic, juicy, and sweet, just like tomatoes, and dried chiles serve much the same purpose as fresh. Cumin is not a traditional spice in pico de gallo, of course, certainly not in the quantity here, but it works astoundingly well in this winter version. Like the summer version on the opposite page, this salsa is delicious with corn tortilla chips or crackers.

1. In a bowl, combine the oranges, onion, chiles, cilantro, cumin, and lime juice. Toss to mix and add salt to taste. Let stand for 15 to 20 minutes, then toss once more and serve.

fava—a creamy yellow split pea puree

Serves 6 to 8

2 cups (390 g) dried yellow split
    peas
¼ cup plus 1 tablespoon (75 ml)
    extra-virgin olive oil
1 teaspoon freshly ground white or
    black pepper
2 to 3 cloves garlic, crushed
1½ cups (190 g) diced onions
2 teaspoons sea salt flakes, plus
    more to taste
1 cup (140 g) shredded carrots
2 to 3 tablespoons lager or water
    for deglazing
2 bay leaves
3 sprigs fresh thyme, or
    ½ teaspoon ground dried
    thyme
1 lemon
Toppings for Summer and Winter
    (recipes follow)

Fava is a dish you can serve warm or at room temperature, but it's also delicious cold. The yellow split pea puree, cut with onions, bay leaves, and thyme and served with different toppings depending on the season, makes a flavorsome and nutritious dish.

1. Put the split peas on a plate and give them a visual check, removing any blackened pieces. Rinse them well in a colander with cold water and let drain.

2. Heat ¼ cup (60 ml) of the olive oil in a large skillet over high heat. Add the pepper and lower the heat to medium-high. Add the garlic and give it a stir with a wooden spoon. Add the onions, and sprinkle the salt over them. Let cook undisturbed for 30 seconds, then mix well and continue to stir until the onions become translucent, a minute or so. Add the carrots.

3. Sauté until the onions soften and turn golden, 5 to 7 minutes. (If they start to stick to the bottom of the pan, add a little lager or water and scrape the bottom of the pan with your spoon, until no lager or water remains.)

4. Add the split peas. Sauté for 1 minute, stirring, and then add 2½ cups (600 ml) water, the bay leaves, and thyme. Turn down the heat to a simmer.

5. Let the split peas cook for 20 minutes, stirring occasionally. Check their progress: Taste to make sure the consistency is soft. If necessary, add more water about ½ cup (120 ml) at a time and cook until they are soft. Finally, squeeze the lemon juice into the pot and give it a good stir. Remove from the heat.

6. Let the fava cool for 10 minutes while you prepare the toppings, then remove the bay leaves and thyme. Use an immersion blender to puree the split peas into a smooth consistency. While mixing, drizzle in the 1 tablespoon of olive oil, as this will help with the mixing and add a little more flavor.

TOPPING FOR SUMMER

½ cup (65 g) diced onion

4 vine-ripened tomatoes, quartered

3 tablespoons capers, drained brined or rinsed salted (and caper leaves if you have them)

Sea salt flakes

Extra-virgin olive oil

TOPPING FOR WINTER

1 tablespoon balsamic vinegar

1 tablespoon honey

¼ cup (60 ml) extra-virgin olive oil, plus 1 tablespoon for drizzling

1 teaspoon freshly ground black pepper

1 cup (80 g) sliced onions

½ teaspoon sea salt flakes

½ pound (225 g) siglino (or substitute good-quality smoked ham, prosciutto, or bacon)

Make the topping

Summer:

1. Top with diced onion, tomato, capers (and caper leaves, if you have them), and salt to taste, drizzle some olive oil on top, and serve.

Winter:

1. In a small bowl, thoroughly mix the vinegar and honey together and set aside.

2. Heat the olive oil in a large skillet over high heat. Add the pepper and lower the heat to medium-high. Add the onions, sprinkle the salt over them, and let cook undisturbed for 30 seconds. Then mix well and cook, stirring for 2 to 5 minutes, until they become translucent. Add the vinegar-honey mixture.

3. Cook for another 10 minutes.

4. Add the siglino and cook for another 5 minutes.

5. Top the fava with the caramelized onions and siglino, drizzle some olive oil on top, and serve.

sea salt and honey hot sauce #3

Makes 4 cups (960 ml)

3 tablespoons extra-virgin olive oil
6 anchovy fillets
4 cloves garlic, minced or pressed
2 to 3 shallots (about 3 ounces/
    85 g) or 1 small onion, minced
1 cup (110 g) grated carrots
2 cups (480 ml) red or white wine
    vinegar
½ cup (120 ml) lager
1 ancho chile
6 amarillo chiles (for extra heat,
    replace with 4 habanero chiles;
    see Tip)
1 dried chipotle chile
2 teaspoons sea salt flakes
2 teaspoons honey

Living in the States for thirty years, I grew accustomed to the heat added to American foods through sauces, such as Tabasco, and Frank's RedHot, used in the coating for buffalo chicken wings. Here is my version of hot sauce using three types of chiles: ancho, amarillo, and chipotle. It will set your kitchen on fire.   —NICHOLAS

1. Pour the olive oil into a small, deep saucepan, add the anchovies, and cook over medium heat, whisking, until the anchovies melt into the oil.

2. Add the garlic and shallots and keep whisking until the shallots become translucent.

3. Add the carrots, then slowly pour in 1½ cups (360 ml) of the vinegar. Raise the heat to high and bring to a boil.

4. Add the lager, chiles, and salt, adjust the heat to medium-low, and simmer for 30 minutes.

5. Remove from the heat and allow the sauce to cool. In a small bowl, mix the honey with the remaining ½ cup (120 ml) vinegar and pour it into the sauce. Use an immersion blender to emulsify everything to a velvety smooth consistency. The color should also appear brighter at this point. If it is too thick, thin with a little more vinegar, to the desired thickness.

TIP: Hot peppers like habaneros and jalapeños, even chipotles, demand a little extra attention: You may want to use rubber gloves when working with them, because no matter how well you wash your hands afterward, you can quite easily inflame anything you touch.

avocado lemon sauce— a healthy hollandaise

Makes about 2 cups (480 ml)

2 ripe avocados
Juice of 1 lemon
¼ teaspoon ground cayenne
    pepper
½ teaspoon sea salt flakes

This is a versatile and healthful sauce to serve on top of eggs, steamed vegetables, dumplings, or to spread on sandwiches.

1. Cut the avocados in half and remove the pits. If you want the true yellow color of hollandaise sauce, scoop only the inner, yellower part of the avocado out and put it in a mini food processor. If you don't mind it turning a little green, use all of the avocado.
2. Add the remaining ingredients and process until smooth.

gorgonzola greek yogurt dip

Makes about 2½ cups (600 ml)

1 cup (135 g) crumbled gorgonzola
    cheese
1 cup (240 ml) whole milk Greek
    yogurt
¼ cup (60 ml) buttermilk
¼ cup (25 g) finely chopped celery

We make this to go with our buffalo wings–style cauliflower and chicken (pages 45 and 204), but it's also excellent as a dip for raw vegetables, pita, and chips.

1. In a bowl, mix all the ingredients together. Cover and chill in the refrigerator for a couple hours before you want to serve it.
2. Store in the refrigerator until ready to use, or for up to 3 days.

feta spreads

Each spread serves 6

These recipes came about after I bought feta and olives at the "olive bar" in a supermarket in the United States. At the olive bar, everything you buy is the same price, so you can, if you like, put different things in the same container and weigh them together. I did just that. When I made our traditional Greek salad that evening, I used half the feta and the olives and the rest stayed in the container, where I also stored a little leftover garlic. The next day, when I went to snack on the feta, I noticed that the cheese had absorbed all the complex flavors of the olives and garlic—and tasted wonderful. So I whizzed some up in the food processor, adding some black pepper, olive oil, and a few capers for good measure. The result was delicious, and I was soon experimenting with sun-dried tomatoes and other peppers and chiles (the second variation, page 71, is similar to the Greek classic tirokafteri). The feta can be used to make dips or spreads and is best served with hot, crusty bread or good crackers.

—NICHOLAS

olive, garlic, and caper feta spread

1 teaspoon chopped fresh garlic

1 cup (150 g) crumbled feta
    cheese, plus more if needed

1 tablespoon capers, drained
    brined or rinsed salted

12 pitted kalamata olives, chopped,
    or 1 tablespoon olive paste

1 teaspoon freshly ground black
    pepper

2½ tablespoons extra-virgin olive
    oil, plus more if needed

¼ cup (60 ml) whole milk Greek
    yogurt (optional; if serving
    as a dip)

1. In a food processor or blender, combine the garlic, cheese, capers, olives, pepper, and olive oil and blend until you have a smooth spread. The consistency should be that of a smooth peanut butter. If the spread is too thick, add more olive oil; if it's too thin, add more cheese until the desired consistency is reached.

2. To make this spread into a dip, add the yogurt.

3. Serve chilled or at room temperature.

pepper and chile feta spread

1 clove garlic, chopped
1 cup (150 g) crumbled feta
    cheese, plus more if needed
1 large red bell pepper, seeded
    and chopped
1 teaspoon chili powder or hot
    pepper flakes
2 tablespoons extra-virgin olive oil,
    plus more if needed
¼ cup (60 ml) whole milk Greek
    yogurt (optional; if serving as
    a dip)

1. In a food processor or blender, combine the garlic, cheese, red bell pepper, chili powder, and olive oil and blend until you have a smooth spread. The consistency should be that of a smooth peanut butter. If the spread is too thick, add more oil; if it's too thin, add more cheese until the desired consistency is reached.

2. To make this into a dip, add the yogurt.

3. Serve chilled or at room temperature.

sun-dried tomato feta spread

1 teaspoon chopped garlic
1 cup (150 g) crumbled feta
    cheese, plus more if needed
1 tablespoon capers, drained
    brined or rinsed salted
¼ cup (14 g) chopped sun-dried
    tomatoes, drained if packed
    in oil
1 teaspoon freshly ground black
    pepper
1 teaspoon dried thyme or oregano
2 tablespoons extra-virgin olive oil,
    plus more if needed
¼ cup (60 ml) whole milk Greek
    yogurt (optional; if serving as
    a dip)

1. In a food processor or blender, combine the garlic, cheese, capers, sun-dried tomatoes, pepper, thyme, and olive oil and blend until you have a smooth spread. The consistency should be that of a smooth peanut butter. If the spread is too thick, add more olive oil; if it's too thin, add more cheese until the desired consistency is reached.

2. To make this spread into a dip, add the yogurt.

3. Serve chilled or at room temperature.

chicken liver pâté flavored with cumin and cilantro

Serves 6 to 8

1 pound (455 g) fresh mizithra or
    Philadelphia cream cheese
2 large eggs, hard-boiled
2 teaspoons freshly ground black
    pepper
Fresh cilantro (coriander) seeds
    (optional; for an extra zing)
1 recipe Chicken Livers with
    Scallions, Cilantro, and Cumin
    (page 208)

If you have cilantro plants in your garden or window box that have gone to seed, this is a great use for those green seeds—they taste like a cross between cilantro leaves and the dried spice coriander.

1. In a food processor or blender, combine all the ingredients, then blend or process until smooth. Transfer to a serving bowl, cover, and refrigerate for at least 2 hours. Serve with crusty bread.

CHAPTER TWO

For Lunch, or to Start an Evening Meal

Fresh
Salads
and
Soups

Ίντα θα φάμε; Τον
άνεμο τηγανιστό και
το βορρά σαλάτα.

What are we going
to eat? The southern
breeze fried and the
north wind salad.

smoked trout and wilted lettuce garden salad

Serves 4

1 head romaine lettuce, leaves separated, long ones torn in half

8 ounces (225 g) smoked trout fillets, cut into ½-inch (12-mm) squares

4 tablespoons (60 ml) fresh lime juice

1 cup (105 g) peeled and thinly sliced kohlrabi

1 cup (20 g) baby arugula

1 cup (45 g) purslane, thicker stems removed

¼ cup (13 g) finely chopped fresh dill

3 tablespoons capers, drained brined or rinsed salted

1 cup (55 g) sliced scallions (white parts ⅛ inch/3 mm thick, green parts ½ to ¾ inch/12 to 20 mm)

6 tablespoons (90 ml) extra-virgin olive oil

1 teaspoon freshly ground black pepper

I used to make this salad and serve it without letting the lettuce wilt. One time, we took it to a party for Chloe's soccer team about an hour away, and when we got there I opened the bowl to see that my crisp lettuce was now wilted. I was going to cover it up and put it back in the car, but I decided to taste it first. To my surprise, it was really good, so I left it on the table. Ten minutes later, several people had asked for the recipe and there was only one bite left in the bowl. So now I always make it an hour ahead of time.

This salad is all about flavor and textural surprises—the velvet of the wilted lettuce, the crunch of the kohlrabi, the tenderness of the trout. The fresh dill and lime offset the smokiness of the trout.

— NICHOLAS

1. In a salad bowl, toss the lettuce, trout, and 1 tablespoon of the lime juice together. Let stand for 30 minutes, tossing periodically. The salt from the trout and the lime juice will start to wilt the lettuce.

2. Add the kohlrabi, arugula, purslane, dill, capers, and scallions and toss. Drizzle the olive oil over the top, along with the rest of the lime juice, sprinkle with the pepper, and serve.

beet salad with apples and greek yogurt

Serves 4

2 to 3 beets, peeled and grated

2 green apples, grated

2 tablespoons golden raisins
   (optional; if using, soak them
   in water overnight so they're
   soft, then drain)

½ teaspoon ground cardamom

½ teaspoon ground cumin

½ cup (120 ml) whole milk Greek
   yogurt, plus more if needed

Beets are in season throughout the year here and take about sixty days to harvest. We use them a lot.

1. In a bowl, toss the beets, apples, raisins (if using), and spices together with ½ cup (120 ml) yogurt, adding more yogurt if necessary to coat the beets and apples. You can make this a couple hours ahead, cover, and store in the refrigerator until ready to serve.

beet and orange salad

Serves 4

2 to 3 beets, cooked, cooled, and
    peeled
3 to 4 oranges, peeled, quartered,
    seeded, and cut into 1-inch
    (2.5-cm) pieces
1 clove garlic, pressed, plus more
    to taste
1 teaspoon sea salt flakes, plus
    more to taste
½ teaspoon freshly ground black
    pepper, plus more to taste
⅓ cup (80 ml) extra-virgin olive oil,
    plus more to taste
3 tablespoons balsamic vinegar,
    plus more to taste
Handful of hulled pumpkin seeds
    (pepitas)
1 to 2 sprigs fresh mint, chopped

This bold and beautifully colored salad is as pretty to look at as it is to eat—delectably sweet and refreshing!

1. Place the beets on a plate (in order to retain all the juices) and cut them into 1-inch (2.5-cm) chunks. Put the beets and any juice from them in a bowl.

2. Add the oranges, garlic (start with 1 clove), salt, pepper, olive oil, and vinegar and stir gently until mixed well.

3. Let the salad sit in the refrigerator for at least 1 hour before serving. (This is a great salad to prepare a day ahead, as the longer the ingredients sit together, the more the flavors meld.)

4. Taste and add more garlic, salt, pepper, or vinegar if needed.

5. Top with pumpkin seeds and mint. Serve cold.

brown lentil salad with radishes, sweet pepper, and caramelized onion

Serves 2 to 4

1⅓ cups (about 8 ounces/225 g) brown lentils (red, green, or yellow work too)

Chicken broth (optional)

¼ cup (60 ml) extra-virgin olive oil, plus more for dressing the salad

1 large onion, sliced

Sea salt flakes

½ teaspoon freshly ground black pepper, plus more to taste

1 yellow bell pepper, sliced

½ bunch fresh parsley, finely chopped in a food processor or with a knife

½ bunch fresh mint, finely chopped in a food processor or with a knife

3 radishes, sliced

2 large cloves garlic, pressed

Juice of 2 lemons, plus more to taste

The combination of deeply caramelized onion and crunchy raw radishes and fresh herbs makes this salad special. Be sure to plan ahead and soak the lentils overnight so they cook evenly.

1. In a bowl, soak the lentils overnight in water to cover. Drain and rinse.

2. Put the lentils in a large saucepan, cover with fresh water (or broth, for more flavor), and boil for 10 minutes, or until soft. Drain and let cool.

3. Heat a large saucepan over medium-high heat and coat the bottom with the ¼ cup (60 ml) olive oil. When the olive oil begins to simmer, add the onion and cook, stirring occasionally, until it begins to turn translucent. Reduce the heat to medium-low, add a pinch of salt and black pepper, and continue to cook, stirring occasionally so the onion doesn't stick to the bottom of the pan, for 20 minutes. If the onions begin to stick, add a little water or broth to the pan. Add the bell pepper and continue to cook, stirring occasionally, until the pepper is soft and the onion is browned, 15 to 20 minutes more. Remove from the heat and let cool.

4. In a large bowl, combine the lentils, onion mixture, herbs, radishes, garlic, lemon juice, and ½ teaspoon salt, stirring until well mixed, then cover and refrigerate for at least 1 hour so the flavors can seep into the lentils.

5. Taste to see if you need to add more salt, black pepper, or lemon juice. Serve cold.

TIPS: This is a great dish to make the day or night before serving. This way the flavors really meld and it comes out nice and cold and refreshing from the fridge.

We know it'd be very easy to throw the garlic in the food processor if you're using one, but we find the garlic stays more chunky, whereas with a press it gets very fine, which is what we prefer in these lentil salads.

COOKING WITH DAD

When I was a child in America, Dad would lift me up onto the kitchen counter so I could look over his shoulder while he cooked. I would watch him crack eggs and whisk them perfectly for omelets or gaze wide-eyed as he added the ingredients to his famous tomato sauce, always teaching and passing on his little wisdoms along the way.

Later on, when I was in college, I'd call him to talk through whatever I was cooking.

"Maybe you should try . . ." he'd say hesitantly, probably sensing an impending disaster.

Dad and I began cooking together seriously when my visits to Kardamili became longer and the gaps in between became shorter. In the beginning it was out of necessity: I was always hungry way before Dad, so in order to get him to start cooking I would wash and chop all the food so it was easy for him to take over. This turned into a lovely routine and I started to gain confidence, and soon there were nights when Dad was prepping the ingredients for me and I was cooking the meal. Now we take turns, and whoever is feeling most inspired—or whoever's stomach is growling the loudest—cooks that evening.

—OLIVIA

lentil salad with sweet pepper, tomatoes, and feta

Serves 2 to 4

1⅓ cups (about 8 ounces/225 g) brown lentils (red, green, or yellow work too)

Chicken broth (optional)

½ cup (70 g) grape tomatoes, halved

1 sweet bell pepper, diced

½ medium red onion, chopped in a food processor or diced

½ bunch fresh basil, finely chopped in a food processor or with a knife

½ bunch fresh mint, finely chopped in a food processor or with a knife

½ teaspoon sea salt flakes, plus more to taste

½ teaspoon freshly ground black pepper, plus more to taste

¼ cup (60 ml) extra-virgin olive oil

¼ cup (60 ml) balsamic vinegar, plus more to taste

¼ pound (115 g) feta cheese

A great summer salad packed with protein, this can easily serve as a full meal. Be sure to plan ahead and soak the lentils overnight so they cook evenly.

1. In a bowl, soak the lentils overnight in water to cover. Drain and rinse.
2. Put the lentils in a large saucepan, cover with water (or broth, for more flavor), and boil for 10 minutes, or until soft. Drain and let cool.
3. In a large bowl, combine the lentils and all the remaining ingredients, stirring until well mixed, then cover and refrigerate for at least 1 hour so the flavors can seep into the lentils.
4. Taste to see if you need to add more salt, black pepper, or vinegar. Serve cold.

TIP: This is a great dish to make the day or night before. This way the flavors really meld and it comes out nice and cold and refreshing from the fridge.

lentil salad with carrots, lemon, and garlic

Serves 2 to 4

1⅓ cups (about 8 ounces/225 g) brown lentils (red, green, or yellow work too)

Chicken broth (optional)

2 large carrots, chopped in a food processor or diced

½ bunch fresh parsley, finely chopped in a food processor or with a knife

½ bunch fresh mint, finely chopped in a food processor or with a knife

2 large cloves garlic, pressed

¼ cup (60 ml) extra-virgin olive oil

Juice of 2 lemons, plus more to taste

2 to 3 tablespoons capers, drained brined or rinsed salted

½ teaspoon sea salt flakes, plus more to taste

½ teaspoon freshly ground black pepper, plus more to taste

Light and refreshing, this salad is great for a hot summer day! Be sure to plan ahead and soak the lentils overnight so they cook evenly.

1. In a bowl, soak the lentils overnight in water to cover. Drain and rinse.
2. Put the lentils in a large saucepan, cover with water (or broth, for more flavor), and boil for 10 minutes, or until soft. Drain and let cool.
3. In a large bowl, combine the lentils and all the remaining ingredients, stirring until well mixed, then cover and refrigerate for at least 1 hour so the flavors can seep into the lentils.
4. Taste to see if you need to add more salt, black pepper, or lemon juice. Serve cold.

TIP: This is a great dish to make the day or night before. This way the flavors really meld and it comes out nice and cold and refreshing from the fridge.

savory greek yogurt bowls

Each recipe serves 2

Savory Greek yogurt bowls are so versatile, always delicious, and best of all easy. You start with your base of a good-quality Greek yogurt and then top it with whatever you have on hand or are craving. Just make sure you include roasted or raw veggies, fresh herbs, a cheese if you'd like, and maybe something crunchy—and always top off with lots of olive oil.

roasted carrot with feta and pistachio yogurt bowl

FOR THE ROASTED CARROTS

⅓ cup (80 ml) honey

1 tablespoon harissa paste

1 teaspoon ground cumin

2 cloves garlic, minced

¼ cup (60 ml) extra-virgin olive oil

2 tablespoons fresh orange juice

1 pound (455 g) carrots, scrubbed (and peeled if you like)

Sea salt flakes and freshly ground black pepper

FOR THE YOGURT BOWLS

1 cup (240 ml) whole milk Greek yogurt

¼ cup (30 g) chopped pistachios

¼ cup (40 g) crumbled feta cheese

¼ cup (13 g) chopped fresh mint

Extra-virgin olive oil

Sea salt flakes and freshly ground black pepper

1. Make the roasted carrots: Preheat the oven to 450°F (230°C).

2. In a large bowl, mix together the honey, harissa paste, cumin, garlic, olive oil, and orange juice.

3. Toss the carrots in the honey mixture to coat, then arrange them in a single layer on a large baking sheet. Season with salt and pepper.

4. Roast 30 to 45 minutes, until the carrots are tender. Let cool.

5. Make the yogurt bowls: Divide the yogurt between two bowls. Top each with the roasted carrots, pistachios, cheese, and mint. Generously drizzle with olive oil. Season with salt and pepper and serve.

herby garden vegetable yogurt bowl

1 cup (240 ml) whole milk Greek
    yogurt
1 tablespoon chopped fresh mint
1 tablespoon chopped fresh basil
1 tablespoon chopped fresh
    oregano
½ cup (90 g) chopped tomato
½ cup (70 g) finely diced
    cucumber
¼ cup (40 g) crumbled feta cheese
Handful of your favorite olives
    (optional), pitted
¼ cup (60 ml) extra-virgin olive oil
Sea salt flakes and freshly ground
    black pepper

1. Divide the yogurt between two bowls. Top each with the herbs, tomato, cucumber, cheese, and olives (if using). Generously drizzle with olive oil. Season with salt and pepper and serve.

BEACH BOUNTY

All of the beaches in Greece are public, and the locals know where to go to find the most delicious seaside edibles. The stretch of beach near the house where I live with my husband, Dimitri, on the grounds of Melitsina, the hotel he owns and runs, has a very different character from most of the others around here. The surface isn't sand or pebbles but a dark gray-black conglomerate that has eroded into an almost lunar texture of small craters and spikes. In summer there's a boardwalk and chairs on the beach for lounging, but it's excellent for foraging year-round.

Sea salt: As the waves crash up and over the rocks, then recede, they deposit pools of salt water in the craters, which evaporates in the sun and leaves behind flaky salt. We just scoop it up and use it as is, with all the flavors of the sea intact, but some folks wash the salt and re-evaporate it: This yields a more neutral (we'd say "less-interesting") flavor and a coarser, crunchier texture. There's an older woman who walks the beach gathering salt to sell to the grocery stores in town—it's not that expensive, about $3 per kilo, so often we'll just buy our salt there and support the local vendors. When Dad goes to a restaurant here in Kardamili, he likes to speculate about who in town collected and processed the salt in the well on the table based on its flavor and consistency.

Kritamo: What looks like tufts of long, thick-bladed grass growing in the conglomerate rock near the salty spray of the crashing waves is kritamo (*Crithmum maritimum*—also known as rock samphire or sea fennel). I like it quick-pickled; Dad prefers it very lightly blanched and served as a salad. It has a mild, fresh, slightly salty sea flavor and is a great source of iodine and other essential minerals.

Capers: A bit farther down the coastline south of Kardamili, in the crevices of rock right on the water, caper bushes (*Capparis spinosa*) flourish. (There are a few bushes on the beach here in Kardamili, but they're more abundant in those southerly spots.) We pick the buds (capers) and sometimes the fruit (caper berries) as well, and pickle them in a simple brine.

—OLIVIA

tuna salad with yogurt, capers, and za'atar

Serves 2

1 (5-ounce/150-g) can tuna in oil,
    drained (or leftover
    grilled tuna)
2 to 3 tablespoons whole milk
    Greek yogurt
1 tablespoon capers, drained
    brined or rinsed salted
3 teaspoons za'atar (page 35)
1 tablespoon extra-virgin olive oil
1 tablespoon apple cider vinegar

This is our spin on the classic American tuna salad. It can be enjoyed plain, with crackers, on a sandwich, or over a bed of crisp lettuce as a salad.

1. In a small bowl, combine all the ingredients together. Serve to your preference.

TIP: To turn this into a tuna melt, turn the oven on to broil. Slice bread of your choice, brush both sides of the slices with olive oil, and place on a baking sheet lined with aluminum foil. Place a hefty scoop of the tuna salad on each slice of bread. Top with the cheese of your choice (feta and halloumi are good options). Broil for 5 to 7 minutes, or until the cheese begins to brown. Serve hot.

horiatiki "village" gazpacho

Serves 4 to 6

1 green bell pepper if making
    Nicholas's version; 2 green
    bell peppers if making Chloe's
    version
1 large onion, cut into large chunks
3 medium to large tomatoes
4 cloves garlic, unpeeled if making
    Chloe's version
¾ cup (115 g) crumbled feta
    cheese, plus more for serving
¼ cup (60 ml) extra-virgin olive
    oil, plus more for serving,
    plus 2 tablespoons if making
    Chloe's version
1 medium cucumber
¼ cup (7 g) fresh oregano, plus
    more for serving
½ cup (75 g) pitted kalamata
    olives, plus more for serving
1 to 2 tablespoons capers, drained
    brined or rinsed salted
½ teaspoon freshly ground black
    pepper
½ teaspoon sea salt flakes (you
    may need more depending on
    how salty your feta is)

We're a huge soup family, but the Kardamili
summer can be quite warm, so we happily resort
to gazpacho. This cold soup combines all the
ingredients of a traditional horiatiki salad blended
together for a refreshing twist on a Greek staple.
We couldn't agree on which version—Nicholas's or
Chloe's—was best, so we've included both!

To make Nicholas's version (all raw):

1. Seed and chop 1 bell pepper. In a food processor
   or blender, combine the bell pepper, onion,
   tomatoes, garlic, and cheese and pulse to finely
   chop. Add the rest of the ingredients and blend
   until smooth. For a thinner soup, add water,
   ½ cup (120 ml) at a time, to desired thickness
   (add no more than 1½ cups/360 ml). Put in the
   refrigerator for at least 4 hours to let the flavors
   develop.

2. To serve, mix well to recombine all the
   ingredients, then divide among bowls and top
   with additional olives, cheese, oregano, and a
   drizzle of olive oil.

To make Chloe's version (some roasted vegetables):

1. Preheat the oven to 400°F (205°C).

2. On a baking sheet, place 2 whole bell peppers, the chopped onion, and the whole garlic cloves with their skin still on. Drizzle 2 tablespoons of olive oil over the onions and garlic, but not on the pepper. Roast for about 30 minutes, tossing the onions occasionally to make sure they don't burn.

3. Once the peppers' skin is blackened and blistered, remove the vegetables from the oven. Put the peppers into a plastic bag or in a bowl covered with a damp paper towel and allow to cool slightly (this will make it easier to peel). Peel, seed, and cut the peppers into strips. Allow the garlic to cool enough to touch with your hands, then squeeze the roasted garlic out of the skin.

4. In a food processor or blender, combine the roasted peppers, onion, and garlic and pulse to finely chop. Add the rest of the ingredients and blend until smooth. For a thinner soup, add water, ½ cup (120 ml) at a time, to desired thickness (add no more than 1½ cups/360 ml). Put in the refrigerator for at least 4 hours to let the flavors develop.

5. To serve, mix well to recombine all ingredients, then divide among bowls and top with additional olives, cheese, herbs, and a drizzle of olive oil.

beet, potato, and ginger soup

Serves 6

2 pounds (910 g) beets, with stems and leaves

1 pound (455 g) new potatoes, washed but not peeled

4 tablespoons (60 ml) extra-virgin olive oil

1 teaspoon freshly ground black pepper

1 cup (90 g) sliced onion

3 teaspoons sea salt flakes

1 tablespoon chopped garlic (2 to 3 cloves)

2 tablespoons finely chopped fresh ginger (see Note)

3 bay leaves

½ cup (120 ml) whole milk Greek yogurt, plus more for serving

1 cup (40 g) chopped fresh cilantro, plus whole leaves for garnish

NOTE: The best way to mince fresh ginger is to slice it across the grain into ⅛-inch (3-mm) coins (so you don't end up with long fibers), and then put it in a food processor or use a sharp knife to finely chop it.

This jewel-colored soup has a rich and velvety texture. Whenever we've served this to beet skeptics they've been completely won over. We love it year-round: In the colder months it can be served hot, with the ginger providing a warm, spicy, and soothing flavor. But it's equally delicious and refreshing served cold in summer topped with yogurt and a few cilantro leaves.

1. Make sure your beets and potatoes are well washed; cut out any bad spots and keep the skins on. Cut the stems off the beets and reserve them.

2. Chop the beets and the potatoes into chunks. Chop the beet stems into 2-inch (5-cm) pieces. You can keep the leaves whole or cut them in half if they are more than 6 inches (15 cm) long.

3. Heat the olive oil in a large pot over high heat. Add the pepper and then lower the heat to medium-high.

4. Add the onion, sprinkle the salt over it, and let cook undisturbed for 30 seconds. Then add the garlic and ginger, mix well, and cook, stirring for about 5 minutes, until the onion is translucent. Add the potatoes and the chopped beets, leaves, and stems. Stir really well and sauté for another 5 minutes, stirring periodically.

5. Add 4 cups (960 ml) water, give a good stir, and add the bay leaves. Turn the heat to high and bring to a boil. Lower the heat to medium-low and simmer, covered, for 35 to 40 minutes, stirring periodically, until the vegetables are tender.

6. Remove from the heat and let cool for 15 minutes. Remove the bay leaves. Using an immersion blender, work the soup into a velvety consistency.

7. Fold in the yogurt and cilantro and stir lightly until well blended. Garnish with a spoonful of yogurt and a sprinkling of cilantro leaves.

roasted carrot and pear soup with ginger and curry spices

Serves 4

1 pound (455 g) carrots, peeled and sliced; julienne 1 carrot for garnish

3 conference or bosc pears, peeled and diced; slice a few pieces for garnish

1 teaspoon sea salt flakes, plus more if needed

4 sprigs fresh thyme

4 tablespoons (60 ml) extra-virgin olive oil

½ teaspoon freshly ground black pepper

1 large onion, chopped

3 cloves garlic, minced

½ cup (95 g) peeled and grated fresh ginger, using a food processor

2 teaspoons garam masala or your favorite curry powder

½ teaspoon chili powder

½ teaspoon grated lemon zest

2 tablespoons fresh lemon juice

½ cup (65 g) pistachios, crushed

For this soup, carrots and pears are roasted to concentrate their sweetness, then blended with garam masala (a combination of spices that's usually heavy on black pepper and cloves for heat), and lemon zest and juice for brightness.

1. Preheat the oven to 400°F (205°C).

2. In a roasting pan, toss the sliced carrots, diced and sliced pears, ½ teaspoon of the salt, and the thyme and drizzle with 1 tablespoon of the olive oil. Roast for 30 minutes, flipping halfway through. When done, remove the thyme sprigs and save them for garnish.

3. Heat the remaining 3 tablespoons of olive oil in a large pot over high heat. Add the pepper and lower the heat to medium-high. Add the onion, sprinkle the remaining ½ teaspoon salt over it, and let cook undisturbed for 30 seconds. Then mix well and cook, stirring for 2 to 5 minutes, until translucent. Add the garlic, ginger, garam masala, chili powder, and lemon zest. Mix everything together and allow to cook for another 5 minutes.

4. Add the roasted carrots and pears and stir well to combine. Sauté for another 5 minutes, stirring periodically.

5. Add 5 cups (1.2 L) water and give it a good stir. Turn the heat to high and bring to a boil. Lower the heat to medium and allow to simmer for 30 minutes, stirring periodically.

6. Remove from the heat and let cool for 5 minutes. Take out 2 or 3 pieces of diced pear and cut into small pieces; set aside to fold into the soup after it's blended.

7. Add the lemon juice to the pot and use an immersion blender to work the soup into a velvety consistency. Add more water if needed. Taste for salt and fold in the chopped, diced pear pieces.

8. Serve in bowls garnished with the roasted pear slices, julienned carrots, pistachios, and the reserved thyme sprigs.

roasted pumpkin soup with coconut milk, ginger, and berbere

Serves 6 to 8

2 pounds (910 g) seeded and peeled pumpkin, cut into rough pieces or slices (start with 2½ to 3 pounds/ 1 to 1.4 kg whole pumpkin); roast the seeds (see Note)

½ cup (120 ml) extra-virgin olive oil, plus more for brushing

3 teaspoons sea salt flakes

2 teaspoons freshly ground black pepper

4 cloves garlic, unpeeled

1 large onion, chopped

½ cup (50 g) thinly sliced peeled fresh ginger (⅛ inch/3 mm slices)

2 teaspoons berbere spice blend (page 35), or more to taste, or curry powder

4 cups (960 ml) vegetable broth

1 (8-ounce/240 ml) can unsweetened coconut milk

The warm spices of berbere, especially the fenugreek seeds with their maple-like fragrance, complement sweet roasted pumpkin beautifully in this smooth cool-weather soup.

1. Preheat the oven to 400°F (205°C).

2. Brush each piece of pumpkin with olive oil, put them in a single layer in a baking sheet, sprinkle each with 1 teaspoon of the salt and the pepper, and tuck the unpeeled garlic cloves among the pumpkin pieces.

3. Roast for 20 to 25 minutes, depending on the thickness of the pieces, until you can easily pierce with a fork. Set aside.

4. Heat the ½ cup (120 ml) of olive oil in a large pot over high heat. Add ½ teaspoon of the pepper and lower the heat to medium-high. Add the onion, sprinkle the remaining salt over it, and let it cook undisturbed for 30 seconds. Then mix well and cook, stirring for 2 to 5 minutes, until translucent. Add the ginger. Make a slit or cut the tip off each clove of garlic and squeeze the roasted garlic into the pot. Give it a stir and add the pumpkin and berbere. Mix well, then continue to sauté for about 10 minutes, stirring often and making sure all the pumpkin is well coated with the seasonings.

5. Add the broth and bring to boil, then lower the heat to medium-low and simmer for 6 minutes. Remove from the heat and let stand for 15 minutes to cool a bit, then add the coconut milk.

6. Using an immersion blender, blend until smooth.

7. Serve in bowls, garnished with the roasted pumpkin seeds.

NOTE: To roast the pumpkin seeds: Preheat the oven to 350°F (175°C). Line a baking sheet with parchment paper. Scoop the seeds out of the pumpkin, removing the stringy fibers, and rinse in a colander. If some of the fibers remain, don't fret; they actually get quite crispy and delicious! Pat the seeds dry with a paper towel. Spread the seeds out in a single layer on the prepared baking sheet. Lightly drizzle olive oil on top, about 1 tablespoon for 1 cup (120 g) seeds. Season with sea salt flakes. We also like to add paprika, piri-piri (page 35), or harissa spice blend (page 35) for a little something extra. Experiment with your favorite seasoning! Bake for 12 to 15 minutes, until the seeds turn golden brown.

chicken soup with egg, lemon, and rice

Serves 6

1 whole uncooked chicken, about
3 pounds/1.4 kg (for traditional
method), or 1 whole cooked
rotisserie chicken (for modern
method)

2 bay leaves

1 sprig fresh sage

2 teaspoons sea salt flakes, plus
more to taste

¾ cup (140 g) Carolina or any long-
grain white rice

3 large eggs

Juice of 2 lemons

TIP: For a creamier soup, whisk
1 tablespoon cornstarch into the
eggs.

The traditional way to start the famous Greek chicken soup called avgolemono is to cook a raw chicken in water to create your own broth while cooking the chicken for the soup. However, sometimes we use a rotisserie chicken instead—we remove the meat, then cook the carcass in water to make the broth. If you're short on time, you can always use good-quality purchased chicken stock.

1. For the traditional method: Put the uncooked chicken in a pot with enough water to cover it by about 1 inch (2.5 cm) (about 6 cups/1.4 L). Add the bay leaves, sage, and salt. Bring to a boil, then lower the heat and simmer for 45 minutes to 1 hour, until the chicken is cooked through. Remove the chicken from the pot and pull the meat from the bones, discarding the bones and skin. Strain the broth and return it to the pot. Place the shredded chicken in the fridge.

   For the modern method: Remove the meat from the cooked rotisserie chicken and set aside in the fridge. Put the chicken carcass and skin in a pot and add about 4 cups (960 ml) water, or enough to submerge it. Add the bay leaves and sage. Bring to a boil, then lower the heat and simmer for about 1 hour. Strain the broth and return it to the pot.

2. Bring the broth to a boil, add the rice, and simmer until the rice is tender, 20 to 30 minutes. Return the chicken meat to the pot and reheat.

3. In a large bowl, beat the eggs and whisk in half of the lemon juice (you can add more lemon to taste later). Take a ladleful of the hot broth and mix it a little at a time into the egg-lemon mixture, while constantly whisking. Continue to add one ladleful of broth at a time until the temperature of the bowl is hot to the touch.

4. Take the pot off the stove. Once the egg bowl is hot, pour the egg mixture into the pot of soup and stir until fully combined. Taste and add more lemon juice if needed and set a small jug of the remaining lemon juice on the table for guests to help themselves. Serve hot.

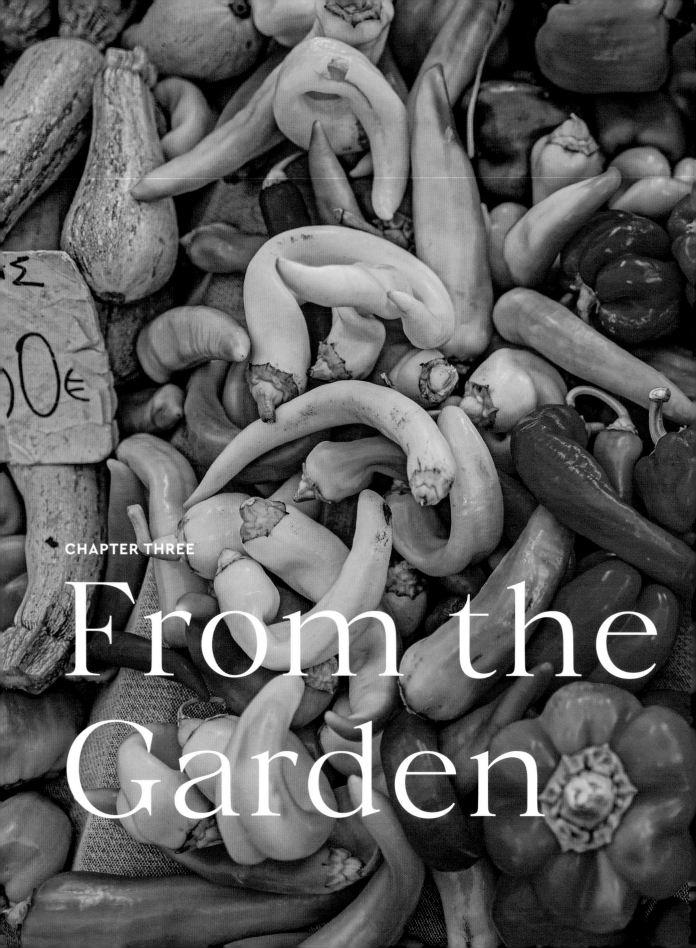

CHAPTER THREE

From the Garden

Seasonal
Vegetable
Sides

Των φρονίμων
τα παιδιά πριν
πεινάσουν
μαγειρεύουν.

Wise children cook
before they are
hungry.

THERE WILL ALWAYS BE A GARDEN

Chloe: For as long as I can remember, our family has had a garden—even when we lived in the middle of the city in Providence, Rhode Island. Dad fenced part of our driveway, dug out the blacktop, filled the area with compost, and we had tomatoes, peppers, cucumbers, carrots, and more. Livi and I were five and three at the time. When we lived in an old farmhouse in the Connecticut countryside, we had a huge vegetable garden. My favorites were the cherry tomatoes that I could pick and eat right off the vine while sitting in the garden. We also had chickens and ducks, and an abundance of eggs with bright orange yolks, unlike anything you'd see in a supermarket egg.

Olivia: I vividly remember the strawberries. Not only because they were delicious but because they were mine—the first things Dad taught me to plant and grow.

Nicholas: At our first house in Kardamili, on a hillside overlooking the village, we planted an extensive garden with more than 160 native and non-native plants— everything from cabbages to coriander, tomatillos to thyme. I recently moved to a place right in town, walkable to everywhere I need to be on a daily basis (the cafés, the beach, the grocery stores) and just a few minutes' walk to Livi and Dimitri's house, and I've already started a garden here—a smaller one this time, but I have the essentials.

Olivia: I put in a garden too, of course—tons of herbs, lettuces, cabbages, onions, and a row of artichokes in front of a stone wall that will look beautiful when they mature. I also planted some sideritis, the flowering herb that grows up in the Taygetos mountains that's dried and used as a tea (see page 262), mostly to see if it grows well here in Kardamili, closer to sea level.

Chloe: I loved working in our family garden as a kid. Now, in New York City, I grow herbs in my apartment and go urban "foraging" for the rest among farmers' markets and specialty shops.

cabbage, carrot, and za'atar slaw

Serves 6

2 cups (190 g) thinly sliced green
    cabbage (1 small head)
2 cups (190 g) thinly sliced purple
    cabbage (1 small head)
1 cup (110 g) shredded carrots
    (2 to 3)
1 cup (240 ml) whole milk Greek
    yogurt
1 tablespoon tahini
1 teaspoon sumac
2 teaspoons sesame seeds,
    toasted
2 teaspoons ground dried thyme
1 teaspoon ground dried oregano
1 teaspoon sea salt flakes

Dried oregano and thyme, sesame seeds, and sumac—the seasoning blend known as za'atar—is one of the most ancient and traditional spice mixtures in the world—in fact Dad insists it's *the* oldest. Za'atar is much more versatile than people give it credit for. Here we use it to transform the all-American coleslaw we miss from home into something more flavorsome; yogurt and tahini instead of the usual mayonnaise makes this a more healthful option too.

If you have za'atar already made and on hand (our recipe is on page 35), use about 2 tablespoons of it here instead of the sumac, sesame, and dried herbs.　　　　　—OLIVIA

1. In a large bowl, mix the cabbages and carrots.
2. In a separate bowl, whisk together the yogurt, tahini, sumac, sesame seeds, thyme, oregano, and salt.
3. Pour the dressing over the vegetables and toss to coat. Refrigerate for 1 hour before serving.

briam with zucchini, eggplant, and tomatoes

Serves 8

5 potatoes, preferably Yukon gold,
    peeled
1 large eggplant
5 medium zucchini
2 large red onions
6 medium tomatoes
1 tablespoon sea salt, plus more
    for the layers
½ cup (120 ml) extra-virgin olive oil
Freshly ground black pepper
1 bunch fresh parsley, stemmed
    and chopped
2 tablespoons dried oregano
4 cloves garlic, thinly sliced
1 (6-ounce/170 g) can tomato
    paste

Briam is a classic dish in which summer vegetables—especially eggplant—are slowly baked in lots of olive oil. It's similar to a French tian, but the bold dose of oregano makes it inescapably Greek.

1. Slice the potatoes, eggplant, and zucchini about ⅛ inch (3 mm) thick. Slice the onions and tomatoes about ¼ inch (6 mm) thick. Layer the eggplant in a dish and sprinkle with ½ teaspoon salt and allow to sit for 30 minutes, then squeeze out excess liquid.

2. Preheat the oven to 350°F (175°C).

3. Pour about ¼ cup (60 ml) of the olive oil in a large baking pan to cover the bottom. Add 1 teaspoon pepper to the olive oil. Layer the sliced potatoes to cover the bottom of the pan. Try to cover all gaps. Sprinkle with some salt, pepper, and one-quarter of the parsley and oregano.

4. Layer the eggplant to completely cover the potatoes. You don't need to salt this layer since it was already salted, but sprinkle with pepper, and one-quarter of the parsley and oregano.

5. Add the zucchini in a layer. Drizzle with 2 tablespoons of olive oil and sprinkle with salt, pepper, and one-quarter of the parsley and oregano.

6. Layer on the onions and the sliced garlic, then top with tomato slices. Sprinkle with salt, pepper, and the remaining parsley and oregano. Drizzle with the remaining 2 tablespoons of olive oil.

7. In a bowl, mix the tomato paste with ½ cup (120 ml) water and pour over the layered vegetables.

8. Bake for 1½ to 2 hours, until all the vegetables are tender (test with a fork). Serve with bread and enjoy.

sautéed string beans with garlic and mustard seeds

Serves 4

¼ cup (60 ml) extra-virgin olive oil
½ teaspoon freshly ground black
    pepper
3 tablespoons mustard seeds
3 cloves garlic, finely chopped
8 ounces (225 g) string beans,
    ends chopped off
1½ teaspoons sea salt flakes

It's amazing how just a few simple ingredients can come together with heat for just a few minutes and deliver so much flavor—especially if you're using fresh homegrown string beans or at least ones bought straight from a farm.

1. Heat the olive oil in a sauté pan over high heat. Add the pepper and lower the heat to medium-high. Add the mustard seeds and garlic and lower the heat to medium-high. Toss in the beans and half of the salt. Cook until the beans are tender but still have a crunch, about 7 minutes. Sprinkle with the rest of the salt and serve.

roasted peppers with anchovies and olives

Serves 6

6 bell peppers (red, yellow, and
    orange), seeded and sliced
4 to 5 cloves garlic, pressed
1 cup (155 g) pitted kalamata olives
½ cup (50 g) dry bread crumbs
½ cup (120 ml) extra-virgin olive oil
1½ teaspoons sea salt flakes
1½ teaspoons freshly ground black
    pepper
1 (2-ounce/56-g) can flat
    anchovies, drained

Slowly roasted peppers, salty olives, and anchovies that melt into the pepper juices and olive oil make this dish irresistible. Serve with crusty bread.

1. Preheat the oven to 350°F (175°C).
2. In a bowl, combine all the ingredients except the anchovies and mix well.
3. Transfer to a baking dish, spread evenly, and lay the anchovies on top.
4. Bake for 45 minutes, then remove from the oven and stir well. Bake for another 15 minutes, or until golden brown. The anchovies should have melted in. Serve hot.

sweet peas with dill and scallions

Serves 2 to 4

¼ cup (60 ml) extra-virgin olive oil
½ teaspoon freshly ground black
    pepper, plus more if needed
2 cloves garlic, minced
6 to 8 scallions, chopped (white
    part ⅛ inch/3 mm thick; green
    part ½ to ¾ inch/12 to 20 mm)
2 teaspoons sea salt flakes, plus
    more to taste
3 pounds (1.4 kg) fresh sweet peas
    in pods, or 2 cups (270 g)
    canned (and drained) or frozen
    peas
½ cup (25 g) fresh dill, finely
    chopped

This dish, loaded with fragrant fresh dill, is extremely versatile: Serve it at any temperature, alongside anything from roast chicken to grilled fish to crusty bread and cheese.

1. Heat the olive oil in a large saucepan over high heat. Add the pepper, reduce the heat to medium-high, and add the garlic, stirring until fragrant, about 1 minute.

2. Add the scallions, sprinkle 2 teaspoons salt over them, and let cook undisturbed for 30 seconds. Stir until the white parts begin to change from white to translucent, 1 minute or so, then let cook for 2 more minutes.

3. Add the peas, stir well, and sauté for 1 minute. If using fresh peas, add warm water to cover them halfway; if they are frozen or canned, add only ½ cup (120 ml) warm water. Add the dill and bring to a boil, then lower the heat to medium-low.

4. Cook until all the water is gone and only the olive oil is left. Season with salt and pepper to taste, then serve hot, at room temperature, or cold.

spiced broccoli florets with pureed stem sauce

Serves 4 to 6

1 large head broccoli, about
   1 pound (½ kg)
2 teaspoons sea salt flakes
3 tablespoons whole milk Greek
   yogurt
2 teaspoons garam masala
⅓ cup (80 ml) extra-virgin olive oil
1 teaspoon freshly ground black
   pepper, plus more to taste
¾ cup (95 g) finely chopped onion
   (about 1 large)
1 teaspoon crushed garlic

Since growing broccoli in our garden we've discovered a way of using every part of this versatile vegetable. If we pick off only the head, the stem continues to sprout smaller florets for a constant supply. We've also found that if the broccoli flowers in a warm spell, it won't go to waste. These delicate yellow flowers have a broccoli taste, with a hint of sweetness. Dotted over salads, they make a tasty and colorful ingredient. This recipe uses the whole broccoli—the florets and thick stem. Don't be put off by the bright green shade. It tastes delicious and packs a serious nutritional punch!

1. Chop the broccoli florets into fine, small chunks. Don't dispose of the stems, but instead dice them, making sure you keep them separate from the broccoli florets. Steam the stems to your preference—we like them steamed for 4 to 6 minutes until fork-tender. Don't drain the water off.

2. Sprinkle 1 teaspoon salt over the stems and let it dissolve, then drain half the water from the pot. Puree the water and the stems with an immersion blender. Add the yogurt and 1 teaspoon garam masala and give it another burst with the blender. Set aside.

3. Pour the olive oil into a pan over high heat and add the remaining 1 teaspoon garam masala and the pepper. Add the onion, giving it a continuous stir. Sprinkle with the remaining 1 teaspoon salt, add the garlic, and lower the heat.

4. Sauté the onion until it has started to soften, then add the broccoli florets and cook for 4 minutes. Put the broccoli and onion mixture in a serving bowl and top it with the pureed stem sauce. Serve.

greens with cannellini beans and garlic

Serves 4

1 pound (455 g) kale or spinach

4 large cloves garlic, pressed

½ cup (120 ml) extra-virgin olive
   oil, plus more for serving,
   if desired

½ teaspoon sea salt flakes, plus
   more to taste

½ teaspoon freshly ground black
   pepper, plus more to taste

1 cup (240 ml) chicken broth

1 (15.5-ounce/480-g) can cannellini
   beans, drained

Pinch of ground cayenne pepper
   (optional)

Easy and delicious, this is a great addition to any meal, and it's ready in minutes! It's also delicious made with escarole or another hearty green. Serve this with crusty bread.

1. Wash the kale, discard the thick stems, and cut the leaves into small pieces.

2. In a large saucepan, combine the kale, garlic, olive oil, salt, black pepper, and broth. Stir and cover.

3. Cook over medium heat until the kale wilts, about 5 minutes, then remove the lid.

4. Add the beans and cook, stirring periodically, until some of the broth has evaporated, about 10 minutes. Taste and season with salt, black pepper, and cayenne (if using). When ready, turn off the heat but leave the pan on the warm burner for 3 minutes. If you'd like, drizzle more olive oil on top. Serve hot.

sautéed spinach with goat cheese and pancetta

Serves 6

½ pound (225 g) pancetta, diced

2 shallots, thinly sliced

4 cloves garlic, minced

1 pound (455 g) spinach

1 lemon, halved

½ cup (75 g) crumbled goat or feta cheese

This easy side dish will delight all your guests and can complement just about any main dish. You can omit the pancetta from this recipe to make it a meatless option by skipping step 1 and cooking the shallots and spinach in 2 tablespoons extra-virgin olive oil over low heat instead. You can also turn this into a breakfast meal by creating wells in the spinach to fry eggs in.

1. In a skillet over medium heat, cook the pancetta, stirring frequently, until it begins to crisp, 8 to 10 minutes. Using a slotted spoon, transfer the pancetta to a paper towel to drain. Leave the rendered fat from the pancetta in the skillet and reduce the heat to low.

2. Add the shallots to the skillet and cook until tender, about 3 minutes. Add the garlic and continue to cook until fragrant, about 2 minutes.

3. Slowly add the spinach to the pan, a handful at a time, adding more as the spinach shrinks and creates more room. Continue until all of the spinach is cooked down.

4. Remove from the heat and squeeze a lemon half over the spinach, adding more lemon juice to taste.

5. Add the cheese and crispy pancetta. Toss everything together and serve.

GREEK FRIES

I don't understand why everyone isn't shouting from the rooftops about the fries in Greece, because they are one of the true wonders of the world. The best are made from potatoes hand-cut into flat, finger-size pieces (kind of like American steakhouse fries) and soaked in cold water for a while to remove some of their excess starch, which will help them crisp up on the outside. They're shallow-fried in olive oil until golden on the outside and fluffy/floury on the inside, then lightly salted and sometimes dusted with dried oregano.

My family doesn't do a lot of frying at home, but when we're out at a restaurant in Greece I will always insist on at least one order of patátes tiganités for the table (if you dip fries into tzatziki, they become more healthful, right?), and I'm sure they silently thank me every time.

—CHLOE

crispy roasted potatoes

Serves 4 to 6

1½ pounds (680 g) potatoes
    (organic, since we will not peel
    them)
Extra-virgin olive oil
2 to 3 cloves garlic, minced
2 to 3 teaspoons sea salt flakes
½ teaspoon freshly ground black
    pepper, plus more to taste
1 to 2 teaspoons berbere spice
    blend (page 35), ras el hanout,
    or dukka

These crisp oven-roasted cubes are the next best thing to real Greek fries—and, with the heat of berbere spices and the bite of garlic, they're quite possibly even more addictive than fried potatoes.

—CHLOE

1. Preheat the oven to 350°F (175°C).

2. Wash and scrub the potatoes and cut them into ¾-inch (2-cm) cubes; it is important that the pieces be the same size so they roast evenly. As you cut them put them in a bowl of water.

3. Stir the potatoes around a few times, change the water, and repeat a couple of times.

4. Brush the bottom of a baking sheet with olive oil. Add the potatoes and garlic and sprinkle with the salt, pepper, and berbere and toss well to coat the potatoes. Arrange in a single layer.

5. Roast for 25 minutes, flip them over, and roast for another 15 to 20 minutes, until golden. Serve hot.

gigantes (giant beans baked in a vegetable sauce)

Serves 6

1 pound (455 g) dried white giant beans

3 teaspoons sea salt flakes, plus more for the beans

2 large or 3 medium onions, chopped

2 carrots, grated

1 to 2 zucchini, grated

1 teaspoon freshly ground black pepper

1 teaspoon berbere spice blend (page 35)

1 cup (240 ml) extra-virgin olive oil

2 cups (480 ml) tomato pulp (if you have fresh vine-ripened tomatoes and a food mill), or 6 tablespoons tomato paste dissolved in 2 cups (480 ml) water

½ cup (25 g) finely chopped fresh parsley

If you have gigantes leftovers, you can puree them for an awesome side dish to go with Lamb Slow-Cooked in the Gastra (page 225) or Sofia's Lemonato Beef (page 216). Be sure to plan ahead and soak the beans overnight so they cook evenly.

1. Put the beans and a handful of salt in a big bowl, cover with enough water to cover the beans twice, and soak overnight.

2. In the morning, remove any loose skins and any that are just about to come off, drain, and put the beans in a gastra.

3. Add all the remaining ingredients except the parsley and mix together.

4. Cover the gastra and put it in a cold oven. Turn the oven on to 350°F (175°C) and bake for 4½ hours.

5. Remove from the oven and let the beans cool in the gastra for 20 minutes, then sprinkle the parsley over and serve.

CHAPTER FOUR

Everyday Meals

Simple Pastas, Risottos, and Lentil Stews

Έφαγα τον κόσμο
να σε βρω.

I ate the whole
world to find you.

harissa and caramelized cabbage over egg noodles

Serves 4

1 teaspoon sea salt flakes, plus
  more for the pasta water
½ cup plus 1 tablespoon (135 ml)
  extra-virgin olive oil
¾ teaspoon freshly ground white
  or black pepper
1 tablespoon crushed garlic
1 medium onion, thinly sliced
¾ teaspoon harissa spice blend
  (page 35)
2 cups (190 g) thinly sliced
  red cabbage
12 ounces (340 g) dried egg
  noodles

Our garden yields an endless supply of cabbages, and their fresh spiciness works beautifully with the hot harissa here. Harissa is an ancient North African spice mix rooted in aromatic Mediterranean herbs that, much like other similar spice mixes in the region, evolved after the arrival of chiles from the Americas and became a fiery blend, one that we happen to love.

1. Bring a large pot of salted water to a boil for the egg noodles.

2. Meanwhile, heat ½ cup (120 ml) of the olive oil in a large skillet over high heat. Add the pepper and lower the heat to medium-high.

3. Add the garlic and give it a stir with a wooden spoon. Add the onion and sprinkle 1 teaspoon salt over it, let cook undisturbed for 30 seconds, then add the harissa and mix well, stirring, until the onion becomes translucent, 1 to 2 minutes.

4. Add the cabbage and cook, stirring continuously, for 2 to 3 minutes, then turn the heat to low. Stir periodically and continue to cook over low heat for about 15 minutes. The cabbage should be well coated with spices and starting to caramelize.

5. Check your pot of water; it should be boiling. Add 1 tablespoon olive oil and the egg noodles. Cook according to the instructions on the package. Drain and divide the egg noodles among four deep plates, top with the caramelized cabbage, and serve.

"BUT WHERE DO YOU SHOP?"

When friends from out of town come to visit, this is always one of the first questions they ask—and that's understandable, given that we live in a village of just a few hundred residents. It's true that shopping—for groceries or any other necessities—takes a bit more forethought and insider knowledge here than it does in the States. We can't just pop out to a suburban-style supermarket or a Target or a big-box home-improvement store. (I think Dad will never fully get used to being without the latter, but he'll survive.)

On the other hand, there are two grocers—for some reason located directly next door to one another—within walking distance of both of our houses. They're small, but carry the essentials: prepared foods and treats (Dad is currently obsessed with these crisp hazelnut cookies, much like biscotti but made from hazelnuts, and meant for dipping into tea), yogurt and cheeses, fresh produce and herbs, olive oil (BYO container or purchase an empty can to fill up), pastas and grains, spices and baking ingredients, cat food, cleaning supplies like the beloved washcloths that Greek people living abroad ask family and friends to send to them, and so on.

In Stoupa, the larger town a few minutes' drive down the coast, there's a legit supermarket—with wide American-style aisles and checkout lanes and everything. That store will special-order ingredients and kitchen wares for you from other parts of Greece or overseas—they've helped us procure certain pans we've needed, as well as delicacies that are harder to come by in Greece, like horseradish sauce. And forty-five minutes up the coast is Kalamata, a good-sized city with pretty much whatever you'd need in the way of groceries and household supplies. Often, though, you might have to go from store to store, because they're fairly specialized: one store for meats, one for dry goods, even one for lightbulbs.

"Okay, but where do you *shop* shop?" Chloe's and my friends from big cities—London, New York, Boston, Athens—are always pleasantly surprised by the incredible variety of super-cute shops along the main street through Kardamili.

Many of them are only open in the warm months, but during the high season we have lots of options for browsing: gift shops selling fine-quality handmade items, the store where we get olive oil (and other excellent olive-adjacent products like soap and olivewood utensils), clothing boutiques, specialty food stores offering mountain honeys and organic baked goods, and more. One of the most common conversational topics in town revolves around what new shops have opened recently—there's always something new to check out in Kardamili.

—OLIVIA

spinach and mushroom penne with garlic and za'atar

Serves 4

2 teaspoons sea salt flakes, plus more for the pasta water

¼ cup plus 1 tablespoon (75 ml) extra-virgin olive oil

1 pound (455 g) dried penne rigate pasta

1 teaspoon freshly ground black pepper

2 tablespoons chopped garlic

1 cup (95 g) sliced mushrooms

2 teaspoons za'atar spice blend (page 35)

1 teaspoon fresh thyme leaves

2 cups (60 g) fresh spinach

3 to 4 sprigs fresh oregano, stems removed

½ cup (50 g) grated parmesan cheese

An exquisite and very easy, very light pasta dish. Seasoned with garlic, black pepper, thyme, oregano, and the za'atar spice blend, the tender spinach and the crisp mushrooms blend with these ancient eastern Mediterranean spices in a symphony of earthy, savory, and citrus flavors.

1. Bring a large pot of salted water to a boil, add the 1 tablespoon of olive oil and the pasta, and cook according to the package instructions minus 30 to 45 seconds. When the pasta is ready, drain and set aside.

2. While the pasta is cooking, heat ¼ cup (60 ml) of the olive oil in a large skillet over high heat. Add the pepper and lower the heat to medium-high. Add the garlic, stir a few times, then add the mushrooms. Cook, tossing and stirring with a wooden spoon, until the edges of the mushrooms start to get crisp, 6 to 8 minutes. Add the 2 teaspoons salt, 1 teaspoon of the za'atar, and the thyme.

3. Add the spinach and toss with everything, cover the pan, and cook for about 2 minutes or until the spinach shrinks down enough for you to stir easily. Uncover, turn the heat to high, and sauté, stirring, until the spinach is wilted and tender, 1 to 2 minutes. Add the pasta to the pan and toss to combine. Sprinkle with the oregano, cheese, and the remaining 1 teaspoon za'atar and serve.

winter garden pasta with purple cabbage, broccoli, cauliflower, sage, and dried chiles

Serves 4

2 teaspoons sea salt flakes, plus
    more for the pasta water
¼ cup plus 1 tablespoon (75 ml)
    extra-virgin olive oil
1 pound (455 g) dried penne
    pasta
½ teaspoon freshly ground black
    pepper, plus more if needed
1 teaspoon chopped garlic
1 to 2 dried chiles, finely
    chopped (hot is better)
¼ cup (9 g) fresh sage leaves,
    chopped
½ pound (225 g) purple
    cabbage, thinly sliced
½ pound (225 g) broccoli florets
¾ to 1 pound (340 to 455 g)
    cauliflower florets
1 cup (115 g) crumbled fresh
    creamy goat cheese

This dish is also great served chilled as a pasta salad. Sometimes we even leave out the pasta altogether and serve the sautéed vegetables and goat cheese as a side dish.

1. Bring a large pot of salted water to a boil, add the 1 tablespoon of olive oil and the pasta, and cook according to the package instructions minus 30 to 45 seconds. When the pasta is ready, drain and set aside.

2. While the pasta is cooking, heat ¼ cup (60 ml) of the olive oil in a deep saucepan over high heat. Add the pepper and lower the heat to medium-high. Stir in the garlic, chiles, and sage and cook until fragrant, about 1 minute.

3. Add the cabbage and 2 teaspoons salt and sauté for 4 to 5 minutes, or until the cabbage shrinks enough to be able to stir in the pan. Add the broccoli and cauliflower, and sauté until the vegetables are your desired tenderness, another 4 to 5 minutes.

4. Remove from the heat, toss in the goat cheese, and mix well.

5. Toss with the pasta and serve.

cauliflower pasta

Serves 4

½ teaspoon sea salt flakes, plus
    more for the pasta water and
    to taste
½ cup plus 1 tablespoon (135 ml)
    extra-virgin olive oil
1 pound (455 g) dried spaghetti, or
    pasta of your choice
1 large head of cauliflower, roughly
    chopped into florets
6 cloves garlic, pressed
Red pepper flakes or a pinch of
    ground cayenne (optional)
¼ teaspoon freshly ground black
    pepper, plus more to taste
4 cups (960 ml) chicken broth
Handful of fresh parsley, chopped
Grated parmesan cheese

Tender cauliflower tangled with pasta sauced with garlicky broth and plenty of good olive oil makes a quick but comforting light meal.

1. Bring a large pot of salted water to a boil, add the 1 tablespoon of olive oil and the pasta, and cook according to the package instructions minus 30 to 45 seconds. When the pasta is ready, drain and set aside.

2. While the pasta is cooking, put the cauliflower, garlic, red pepper flakes (if using), and ½ cup (120 ml) of the olive oil in a large skillet over medium heat. Sauté until the garlic is fragrant, stirring often to keep the garlic from burning, a few minutes.

3. Add the ½ teaspoon salt, the black pepper, and 2 cups (480 ml) of the broth. Turn the heat to medium-high and bring to a boil. Cover the pan and lower the heat to medium. Simmer until the cauliflower is fork-tender, about 10 minutes.

4. Add the remaining 2 cups (480 ml) broth and begin to break up the cauliflower with a wooden spoon. Bring back to a boil and simmer until fully tender, another 5 to 7 minutes.

5. Add the pasta to the pan with the cauliflower and mix together. Top with the parsley and more salt and pepper to taste. Serve with lots of parmesan cheese.

zucchini, siglino, and sage pasta

Serves 4

1 teaspoon sea salt flakes, plus
    more for the pasta water
⅓ cup plus 1 tablespoon (95 ml)
    extra-virgin olive oil
1 pound (455 g) dried pasta, such
    as rigatoni
1 teaspoon freshly ground black
    pepper
2 teaspoons chopped garlic
½ cup (45 g) thinly sliced onion
⅓ cup (20 g) scallions, chopped
    (white parts ⅛ inch/3 mm
    thick, green parts ½ to
    ¾ inch/12 to 20 mm)
¾ teaspoon ground dried sage
1 cup (160 g) cubed siglino (or
    substitute good-quality
    smoked ham, prosciutto, or
    bacon)
2 cups (230 g) thinly sliced
    zucchini
Grated parmesan cheese

Zucchini are a regular part of our diet, not only because we harvest a never-ending crop between the months of June and September, but also because we love them. Greeks prepare zucchini in several different ways—including crispy fried or stuffed. We created this dish with aromatic sage, plucked from the mountains above Kardamili and dried in our kitchens, and the local cured smoked pork, siglino. The saltiness of the pork complements the sweetness of the vegetables. We eat this on its own as an appetizer or on top of pasta for a main meal, as here.

1. Bring a large pot of salted water to a boil, add the 1 tablespoon of olive oil and the pasta, and cook according to the package instructions minus 30 to 45 seconds. When the pasta is ready, drain and set aside.

2. While the pasta is cooking, heat the ⅓ cup (80 ml) of the olive oil in a large skillet over high heat. Add the pepper and lower the heat to medium-high. Stir in the garlic and cook until fragrant, about 2 minutes.

3. Add the onion and scallions, sprinkle the 1 teaspoon salt over them, and let cook undisturbed for 30 seconds, then add the sage and stir well. Cook, stirring often, until the onions are golden brown, 4 to 5 minutes.

4. Add the siglino and zucchini and stir for 2 minutes, then turn the heat to low and cook for 4 minutes longer.

5. Spoon the vegetable mixture over the pasta, top with cheese, and serve.

linguine with siglino, mushrooms, and peas in a greek yogurt sauce

Serves 4

2 teaspoons sea salt flakes, plus
more for the pasta water
¼ cup plus 1 tablespoon (75 ml)
extra-virgin olive oil
1 pound (455 g) dried linguine
pasta
1 cup (145 g) fresh or frozen peas,
rinsed
1 teaspoon freshly ground black
pepper, plus more to taste
3 cloves garlic, pressed
6 to 7 white button mushrooms
½ pound (225 g) siglino (or
substitute good-quality
smoked ham, prosciutto, or
bacon), sliced
2½ cups (600 ml) whole milk Greek
yogurt
3 large eggs
Grated parmesan cheese

I was craving carbonara one night and used the
ingredients we had at home to come up with
something similarly creamy and comforting.

—OLIVIA

1. Bring a large pot of salted water to a boil, add
   the 1 tablespoon of olive oil and the pasta, and
   cook according to the package instructions,
   adding the peas to the boiling water when
   there is about 5 minutes left to the pasta
   cooking time.

2. Once the pasta is cooked, save about 2½ cups
   (600 ml) of the pasta water (best to have a little
   extra) and drain the rest, then return the pasta
   and peas to the pot. Set aside.

3. Meanwhile, heat ¼ cup (60 ml) of the olive
   oil in a large skillet over high heat. Add the
   pepper and lower the heat to medium-high,
   then add the garlic and cook until fragrant. Add
   the mushrooms and 2 teaspoons salt. Cook
   for about 6 minutes, until they shrink. Add the
   siglino and sauté for 2 minutes, then lower the
   heat to medium.

4. Meanwhile, in a bowl, combine the yogurt and
   the eggs, mixing well. When completely mixed,
   gradually add 1½ cups (360 ml) of the pasta
   water, whisking constantly.

5. Pour the yogurt mixture over the mushrooms
   and siglino and cook for another 2 minutes,
   stirring constantly; if it looks as though you will
   need more pasta water to make the sauce more
   liquidy, add ½ cup (120 ml) now, stir, and cook
   for 1 more minute.

6. Pour the sauce over the pasta and peas and toss
   well. Top with cheese and serve.

beet and goat cheese risotto with pistachios and scallions

Serves 4

4 cups (1 L) chicken broth

2 tablespoons extra-virgin olive oil

1 cup (125 g) finely chopped onion

1½ cups (285 g) arborio rice

2 cloves garlic, finely chopped

1 cup (240 ml) white wine (optional)

3 roasted beets, peeled and chopped

½ cup (55 g) crumbled goat cheese

¼ cup (25 g) grated parmesan cheese

Sea salt and freshly ground black pepper

2 scallions, chopped (white parts ⅛ inch/3 mm thick, green parts ½ to ¾ inch/12 to 20 mm)

¼ cup (30 g) pistachios, chopped

Roasted beets and goat cheese are a classic combination, expressed here as a beautiful pink risotto made in the traditional way: sautéing the rice, then adding liquids a little at a time, stirring all the while. A shower of fresh scallions and crunchy pistachios adds texture and color.

1. In a medium saucepan, bring the broth to a simmer.

2. In a large skillet, heat the olive oil over medium heat. Add the onion and sauté until it becomes soft and golden, about 5 minutes. Move the onion toward the outside edge of the pan and add the rice to the center. Sauté the rice until the grains become translucent, about 3 minutes. Mix the onions in with the rice and toss in the garlic. Stir until the garlic becomes fragrant, about 2 minutes.

3. If using wine, add it to the pan while scraping everything from the bottom and mixing it all together. Adding the liquid will cause the pan to steam up, but continue to stir. As the wine is absorbed, begin to add simmering broth to the pan, one ladleful at a time, stirring in between each addition. Repeat until all the broth has been added and absorbed and the rice is tender, continuing the process with hot water if you run out of broth before the rice is fully tender, about 30 minutes total.

4. Add the beets and mix well.

5. Remove from the heat, add both cheeses, and cover the pan. Allow to sit for 2 to 3 minutes so the cheeses can melt before mixing. Uncover, mix well, and add salt and pepper to taste.

6. Top with the scallions and pistachios and serve.

mushroom and beef broth risotto

Serves 4

4 cups (1 L) beef broth, plus more if needed
2 tablespoons extra-virgin olive oil
1 medium onion, diced
¾ pound (340 g) cremini or button mushrooms, finely chopped
1½ cups (285 g) arborio rice
3 cloves garlic, minced
1 teaspoon chopped fresh thyme
1 teaspoon chopped fresh sage
½ cup (50 g) grated parmesan cheese
Sea salt and freshly ground black pepper

Lots of earthy mushrooms, thyme, and sage make this hearty risotto the perfect dish for fall. Swap out the beef broth for a rich vegetable broth and serve with mixed roasted vegetables for a satisfying vegetarian meal.

1. In a medium saucepan, bring 4 cups (1 L) of the broth to a simmer.

2. In a large skillet, heat the olive oil over medium-high heat. Add the onion and mushrooms and sauté until tender, 5 to 7 minutes.

3. Move the mixture toward the outside edge of the pan and add the rice to the middle. Sauté the rice, stirring constantly, until the grains become translucent, about 3 minutes. Mix the onion and mushrooms in with the rice and toss in the garlic and herbs. Cook until the garlic becomes fragrant, about 2 minutes.

4. Begin to add just enough simmering stock to cover the ingredients, a ladleful at a time, while scraping up any bits sticking to the bottom. Adding the initial liquid will cause the pan to steam up, but continue to stir. As the liquid is absorbed, continue to add more stock, one ladleful at a time, stirring in between, until the rice is tender. Add more broth or water if you run out before the rice is tender.

5. When the rice is tender, remove from the heat, add the cheese, and put a lid on the pan. Allow to sit for 2 to 3 minutes so the cheese can melt before mixing. Remove the lid, mix well, and add salt and pepper to taste. Serve hot.

stewed lentils with carrots, zucchini, and tomatoes

Serves 6 to 8

1 pound (455 g) brown lentils (red, green, or yellow work too)
¼ cup (60 ml) extra-virgin olive oil
1 teaspoon freshly ground black pepper, plus more to taste
2 onions, diced
6 cloves garlic, 3 sliced and 3 pressed
1½ teaspoons sea salt flakes
4 carrots, cut into half moons
2 to 3 ribs celery (optional), chopped
2 medium zucchini, cut into half moons
1 (14.5-ounce/480-g) can crushed tomatoes
2 quarts (2 L) chicken stock
Feta cheese

This is true comfort food, with a few twists: These satisfying lentils feature onions and carrots, plus tender zucchini, the tang of tomatoes, and a generous dose of bright and salty feta. Put a sliced loaf of crusty bread on the table and call it a meal. Be sure to plan ahead and soak the lentils overnight so they cook evenly.

1. In a bowl, soak the lentils overnight in water to cover. Drain, rinse, and set aside.

2. Heat the olive oil in a large pot on high heat. Add 1 teaspoon of the pepper and lower the heat to medium-high. Add the onions and sliced and pressed garlic, sprinkle ½ teaspoon of the salt over them, and cook undisturbed for 30 seconds. Mix well and sauté until translucent and golden, another 5 to 7 minutes.

3. Add the carrots, celery (if using), and zucchini to the pot, stir well, and add ½ teaspoon salt. Cook until the vegetables begin to soften, about 4 minutes.

4. Add the lentils to the pot as well as the remaining ½ teaspoon salt, and sauté for 2 minutes, stirring continuously.

5. Add the tomatoes, stir, and cook for 1 minute.

6. Add the stock, bring to a boil, then lower the heat, cover, and simmer for a minimum of 2 hours, stirring occasionally. If it seems the liquid will disappear before the 2 hours, add water 1 cup (240 ml) at a time.

7. Taste for salt and pepper and add more if needed. When the lentils start to thicken up, the stew is ready. (If you had to add water, this may take longer than 2 hours.)

8. Serve with feta cheese; we like to top our bowls with it.

lentil chili slow-cooked with beer

Serves 6 to 8

1 cup (190 g) brown lentils (red, green, or yellow work too)
¼ cup (60 ml) extra-virgin olive oil
2 teaspoons freshly ground black pepper
1 tablespoon chopped garlic
2 cups (250 g) diced onion
2 teaspoons sea salt flakes, or more to taste
3 teaspoons ground cumin
1 teaspoon chili powder
¾ cup (180 ml) pale ale
2 cups (480 ml) canned crushed tomatoes
1 teaspoon dried oregano
⅔ cup (25 g) chopped fresh cilantro
Juice of 2 limes
1 cup (115 g) coarsely shredded cheddar cheese (1 to 2 tablespoons per serving)
1 cup (240 ml) whole milk Greek yogurt (1 to 2 tablespoons per serving)

This recipe draws on Minoan roots, using herbs like cilantro, which was used in the Bronze Age but is rarely used in Greek cooking these days. Boiling in beer, too, was common practice. Of course, the Minoans would have had their dish simmering away in large clay pots on an open hearth.

For our dish, it's better to use a premium pale ale rather than a lager. We sometimes eat the chili by scooping it up with tortilla chips, but serving it with rice or crusty bread is equally delicious. The chili can also be cooked well in advance and reheated, allowing the flavors time to develop. Be sure to plan ahead and soak the lentils overnight so they cook evenly.

1. In a bowl, soak the lentils overnight in water to cover. Drain and rinse.

2. Heat the olive oil in a large skillet over high heat. Add the black pepper and lower the heat to medium-high. Stir in the garlic and cook until fragrant, about 1 minute. Add the onion, sprinkle 2 teaspoons of flaky salt over it, and let it cook undisturbed for 30 seconds. Add the cumin and chili powder. Mix well and sauté until the onions are translucent and golden and all their excess water has evaporated, 5 to 7 minutes.

3. Add the lentils and sauté for another 6 minutes. If the lentils start to stick, pour in a drop of the beer and stir. Add the tomatoes, then slowly pour all of the beer into the pot, stirring gently as you go. Once the liquid begins to boil, lower the heat to a gentle simmer. Add the oregano and stir.

4. Simmer for 40 to 45 minutes. Keep checking until the chili is thick and most of the liquid is gone. Stir in the cilantro and lime juice.

5. Serve hot. Top with cheese and yogurt or serve the accompaniments on the side to complement the hot chili.

CHAPTER FIVE

From the Sea

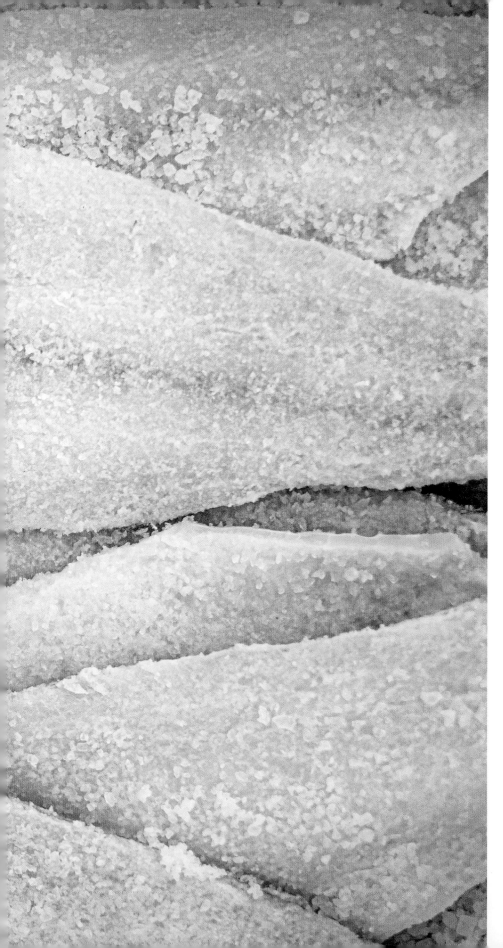

Baked, Grilled, Sautéed, and Parchment-Wrapped

Κάθε πράγμα
στον καιρό του
κι ο κολιός τον
Αύγουστο.

Everything in time
and the mackerel in
August.

calamari slow-cooked in the gastra

Serves 4 to 6

3 to 4 potatoes, preferably Yukon gold, cut into ¾-inch (2-cm) cubes

1 large onion, chopped

2 cloves garlic, thinly sliced

2 scallions, chopped (white parts ⅛ inch/3 mm thick, green parts ½ to ¾ inch/12 to 20 mm)

½ cup (120 ml) extra-virgin olive oil

2 teaspoons sea salt flakes

2 teaspoons freshly ground black pepper

1 teaspoon ground cumin

2 pounds (910 g) calamari, cleaned

½ cup (25 g) finely chopped fresh parsley

The old rule of thumb is that for maximum tenderness, calamari should be cooked for either thirty seconds or thirty minutes. We would modify that rule to say that if you're baking it in a traditional clay gastra, *three hours* is ideal.

1. Put the potatoes, onion, garlic, scallions, olive oil, salt, pepper, and cumin in a gastra and mix well so everything gets coated.

2. Push the ingredients to the edges of the pot so there's space in the center, then pour 2 cups (480 ml) water into the space and add the calamari to the water.

3. Cover the gastra, put it in a cold oven, and turn the oven to 350°F (175°C). Bake for 3 hours. All the liquid except the olive oil should be gone; if not, put the gastra back in the oven uncovered and bake for 10 to 20 minutes.

4. Sprinkle the parsley over and serve.

dirty shrimp

Serves 4

Scented with fennel seeds and a healthy dose of raki, then brightened with a last-minute squeeze of lime, these shrimp cook up quickly for an easy light supper or appetizer.

2 pounds (910 g) fresh whole red shrimp (also called Mediterranean or Argentinian shrimp), or shell-on regular shrimp
3 tablespoons extra-virgin olive oil
½ teaspoon freshly ground black pepper
1 large onion, finely chopped
1 teaspoon sea salt flakes
2 teaspoons fennel seeds
½ cup (120 ml) raki (or ouzo, tequila, or vodka)
Juice of 1 lime

1. Put the shrimp in a colander and rinse well under running water; set aside to drain.
2. In a large frying pan, heat the olive oil over high heat. Add the pepper and lower the heat to medium-high. Add the onion, sprinkle on the salt and fennel seeds, and let cook undisturbed for 30 seconds, then stir well and sauté for 2 minutes.
3. Add the shrimp, stir to coat the shrimp well with the onion, and sauté for 2 minutes.
4. Add the raki, lower the heat to medium, and cook for a few more minutes, until most of the liquid is gone.
5. Drizzle with the lime juice, remove from the heat, and serve.

fish dolmades

Serves 4 to 6

FOR THE DOLMADES

24 romaine lettuce leaves
(1 to 2 heads)
2 medium onions
1 cup (4½ ounces/130 g) chopped
fresh cod fillet
1 cup (190 to 195 g) long-grain
white rice
½ cup (25 g) chopped fresh
parsley
½ cup (25 g) chopped fresh dill
2 tablespoons extra-virgin olive oil,
plus more if needed
1 teaspoon freshly ground black
pepper, plus more to taste
1 tablespoon sea salt flakes

FOR THE EGG-LEMON SAUCE

2 large eggs
Juice of ½ lemon
1 tablespoon cornstarch

There are many traditional ways to stuff dolmades—with lamb or beef or a variety of vegetables. But one day when I was in a taverna, I ordered dolmades expecting the usual, took my first bite, and was pleasantly surprised to discover it had been filled with fish. I set out to re-create this recipe at home, and the result was worth the effort. We use romaine lettuce leaves to parcel our ingredients since we can grow lettuce almost all year, but cabbage leaves or fresh or vacuum-packed vine leaves work well too. Despite it being considered a cold-water northern European fish, cod is very popular in the Peloponnese, in particular salted cod, which the Greeks call "mountain fish," often served in tavernas. However, overfishing has made it more difficult to buy fresh cod here, so we use any tender, white flaky fish as an alternative. Salmon can also be used.

—NICHOLAS

1. Make the dolmades: Wash the lettuce leaves, then blanch them by dipping them in boiling water for 45 to 60 seconds. Set aside.

2. Using the largest holes on a box grater, grate the onions. In a bowl, combine the onions, cod, rice, parsley, dill, 2 tablespoons of the olive oil, the pepper, and salt and mix together by hand. If it's too dry, add another tablespoon of olive oil.

3. Scoop 1 tablespoon of the mixture into the large part of a lettuce leaf—the raised lettuce vein should be on the inside of the roll—and roll for a few turns, then fold in the sides. Continue rolling all the way up to the end and set aside. Repeat with the remaining filling and lettuce.

4. Line the base of a small round pot with the dolmades, covering the surface and then stacking them in layers. Pour in 2 cups (480 ml) water, bring to a boil, then lower the heat and gently simmer for 40 minutes. It's a good idea to place a heavy plate on top of the dolmades as they cook, to keep them in place.

5. Meanwhile, make the egg-lemon sauce: In a bowl, beat the eggs, adding the lemon juice and cornstarch.

6. When the dolmades are cooked, ladle some of the hot liquid from the pot into the egg mixture in small amounts, stirring constantly (add the liquid until the bowl feels hot to the touch). Pour the sauce over the dolmades and serve.

baked cod with orange, onion, capers, and thyme in parchment parcels

Serves 4

4 (4½-ounce/130-g) cod fillets
1 teaspoon freshly ground black
     pepper
1 orange, one half cut into at least
     8 thin slices and the other left
     intact
1 medium onion, sliced
1 teaspoon sea salt flakes
4 teaspoons capers, drained
     brined or rinsed salted
½ cup (120 ml) extra-virgin olive oil
1 to 2 teaspoons fresh thyme

Baking in sealed parchment paper packets keeps fish moist and traps all the aromas of the herbs and other ingredients until the packets are (carefully) opened at the table.

1. Preheat the oven to 400°F (205°C).

2. Place each cod fillet onto a generously sized piece of parchment paper. (Make the pieces of paper large enough so that they will be easy to roll, fold, and seal.)

3. Sprinkle with the pepper—about ¼ teaspoon on each fillet. Place at least 2 orange slices on each fillet. Use all your slices; they don't all need to be on top of the fillet; some could be quartered and placed in the parcel.

4. Fill in the gaps between the orange slices with slices of onion. You want some onion to be directly on the fillet and some around it in the parcel.

5. Sprinkle with the salt—about ¼ teaspoon on each fillet. Spoon 1 teaspoon capers on each fillet, distributing them evenly throughout the parcel. Drizzle 2 tablespoons of olive oil on each fillet.

6. Sprinkle with the thyme—¼ to ½ teaspoon on each fillet.

7. To seal the parcels, bring the long sides together, then roll all the way down. Then roll in each side, folding in and tucking the corners. To really make sure no steam escapes, wrap the parchment parcel in aluminum foil. Place on a baking sheet and bake for 25 minutes.

8. Open the parcels at the table.

salmon masala
with wild rice

Serves 4

FOR THE MARINADE

2 cups (480 ml) whole milk Greek
  yogurt

¼ cup (10 g) finely chopped fresh
  cilantro, plus 4 sprigs for
  garnish

1 teaspoon ground cardamom

1 teaspoon ground coriander

1 teaspoon ground cumin

1 teaspoon ground turmeric

1 teaspoon ground cayenne
  pepper

2 tablespoons minced garlic

3- to 4-inch (7.5- to 10-cm) piece
  of fresh ginger, minced (see
  Note, page 97)

1½ teaspoons sea salt flakes

FOR THE SALMON

4 (6-ounce/180-g) skinless,
  boneless salmon fillets

FOR THE RICE

1 tablespoon extra-virgin olive oil

1 cup (175 g) wild rice

2 cups (480 ml) salted chicken
  broth, or 2 cups (480 ml) water
  and 1 teaspoon sea salt flakes

Salmon is a delicate and mild-flavored fish, and we love it simply grilled with salt, olive oil, and a squeeze of lemon, but sometimes we crave bolder interpretations like this one. Here the fish is marinated in cardamom- and curry-spiced yogurt and served with a wild rice whose nutty flavor stands up well to the spices.

1. Make the marinade: In a container big enough to hold the salmon and the yogurt, mix the yogurt with all the marinade ingredients. After it's mixed, take 1 cup (240 ml) of the marinade out.

2. Layer the salmon fillets on top of one another in the container, spooning some of the reserved marinade between the layers. If there is any marinade left, pour it on top. Cover and refrigerate for at least 4 hours.

3. If baking the salmon, preheat the oven to 425°F (220°C) and line a baking sheet with aluminum foil. If you are grilling, preheat the grill.

4. Make the rice: In a saucepan over high heat, combine the olive oil and rice and sauté for 2 minutes. Add the broth, bring to a boil, then lower the heat and simmer according to the instructions on the rice package.

5. When the rice has about 15 minutes left, arrange the salmon fillets on the prepared baking sheet and bake for 10 to 12 minutes, using some of the marinade to baste the fish several times. Reserve the remaining marinade. Broil for the last 2 minutes. If using the grill, cook the salmon for 4 to 5 minutes per side. The fish is done when flaky.

6. Meanwhile, in a pan over medium-low, heat the remaining marinade to make the sauce. Cook, stirring frequently, for 6 to 8 minutes, then remove from the heat and let stand until the salmon and rice are done.

7. Serve the salmon and rice on a dish, pour the sauce over both, and garnish with cilantro sprigs.

MINOAN SPICE

I've always been fascinated by the foodways of ancient Greece, in particular the Minoan civilization on Crete, the large island just to the southeast of the Peloponnese. The Minoans thrived for nearly six centuries until the civilization's decline following the devastating eruption of the volcanic island of Thera sometime in the middle of the second millennium BCE. Archaeological remains have given us a detailed picture of the meats, cultivated grains, and other proteins the Minoans ate, and how they were cooked. But it's harder to know what those foods might have tasted like, because evidence of the use of delicate ingredients like herbs and spices are less prevalent in the archaeological record.

This is why the tablets containing Linear B text—a script that predates ancient Greek—and their decipherment in the mid-twentieth century has been so important to food anthropologists. From these clay tablets, which are extant today only because they were preserved like rudimentary pottery in fires in the archives of what were thought to be palaces (but might not have been) around 1200 BCE, we can see that Bronze Age Cretans were using spices like coriander, cumin, fennel, sesame, cardamom, mustard, horseradish, and saffron that are native to the area as well as spices they would acquire through trade from Persia, India, and Africa— flavors most people wouldn't readily associate with "traditional" Greek cooking today. Perhaps the liberal use of all of these flavors in our own kitchens isn't as far a stretch as it might seem.

If you visit Athens, be sure to stop at the National Archaeological Museum and seek out the generous display of Linear B tablets and frescoes. The Minoan frescoes in particular show a love of life, animals, sea and plant life, and games—and demonstrate the prominent role women played in the Minoan culture. Interestingly, the frescoes do not feature weapons or wars or hunts, suggesting that Minoan Crete (unlike later periods in the rest of Greece) was a peaceful, highly advanced society. Crete, an island of fiercely independent people today, was clearly ahead of its time as early as the Bronze Age.

—NICHOLAS

OLIVIA'S BEACH GUIDE

All of these extraordinary beaches are within a fifteen-minute drive of Kardamili.
Roughly from north to south:

Ritsa: Closest to home is Ritsa beach, and Chloe, who is never happier than when
she's relaxing on a lounge chair at Ritsa with an order of keftedes, fries, and tzatziki
from nearby Kelly's (officially Ta Ritsa—τα Ρίτσα), would say that Dad and I take
it for granted, but we really don't. Every hour we spend on this smooth-pebbled
beach, just a few steps from each of our houses, is treasured. It has a laid-back
vibe, with a handful of restaurants we frequent on rotation: Gialos (Γιαλός), where
we usually go once a week in the summer for live music in the evening; a cute
cantina called Mono Votsalo (Μόνο βότσαλο); Galazio (Γαλάζιο), Dad's summer
office and where I get my favorite iced tea; Elies (Ελιές), which serves delicious
traditional Greek food with hefty portions; Melitsina's Xai Xou (Μελίτσινα Xai Xou),
which emphasizes local ingredients and features a few of *Sea Salt and Honey*'s
recipes on the menu. They also serve excellent cocktails and it is our favorite place
to watch the full moon rise. The southern end of Ritsa is especially popular with
surfers: It's regularly named on top-ten lists of surfing spots in Greece.

Kalamitsi: This is the beach made famous by British author Patrick Leigh Fermor—
his stone house sits just above it, tucked discreetly behind a grove of olive and fig
trees, and from here you have a perfect view of tiny Meropi island, close enough to
swim out to. A high cliff punctuated by tall cypress trees serves as a backdrop to
the south of the beach of smooth, fist-size stones.

Foneas: This is Dad's favorite beach, and it's certainly the most dramatic looking,
situated in a narrow horseshoe surrounded by steep hills; a winding trail leads
down to the beach from the main road. In the center of the horseshoe a huge rock
juts out of the water, and brave kids and adults climb up and jump off it into the
bright blue sea. In summer, an easygoing cantina serves up snacks and drinks so
you can stay all day, lounging on the mixed sand-and-pebble beach.

Delfinia: Just a minute or two down the coast is Delfinia ("dolphin"), and it's
probably my own favorite. It's hugged by cliffs, like Foneas, but its inward curve is

gentler, so it's quieter and more peaceful than echo-y Foneas, even when there are other people around. It's the ideal spot to pitch a lounge chair at dusk, when the sun sinks down behind the water straight out in front of you in the bay.

Kalogria: Now we're getting into more developed territory. Walk down from the main road into Stoupa, past a grayscale mural of the late local author Nikos Kazantzakis and his most famous character, Zorba (the Greek), and you'll find a bustling beach scene. Kalogria draws a younger, more social crowd: There are volleyball nets set up on the fine white sand, cafés with outdoor seating under eucalyptus trees, and a wealth of cushioned lounge chairs, umbrellas, and hammocks. The water is shallow far out into the bay, and a little cooler than at other beaches nearby, as undersea springs deliver fresh water from high in the mountains.

Stoupa: The main drag of this village, which is a bit larger than Kardamili, is situated by the water, with restaurants and shops on one side and the sandy beach on the other. It gets a little crowded in the high season, and is especially popular with British tourists. At the far north end, there's a beach that's only really accessible from the property of the restaurant above it, so it's quieter and more "private." At the southern end, there's an establishment with a beautiful roof bar where we like to have cocktails in the evenings.

Agios Nikolaos: This small fishing community named after St. Nicholas is much less touristy than Stoupa, the village just north of it, and it's livelier in the wintertime because there are more permanent residents here. A microbrewery just opened up near the main road, and there are at least two top-notch seafood restaurants facing the small piers where the fishing boats offload their catch. Toward the far end of town is Pantazi beach, and at the far end of Pantazi is a little nook hidden behind some rocks that's known as "the kissing beach," for reasons that are probably obvious.

Farther down the Mani coast are a few more favorite spots—where we kayak or swim into seaside caves, or float in the warm, calm waters that wash into a natural stone pool at the edge of the waterline—but I'll let you discover special places like those for yourself.

grilled octopus marinated in red wine vinegar, honey, and oregano

Serves 4

1 (2- to 3-pound/910-g to 1.4-kg)
   fresh octopus, cleaned by your
   fishmonger (unless you are
   very brave and you know how
   to clean it)
½ cup (120 ml) honey
1 teaspoon sea salt flakes
½ cup (120 ml) red wine vinegar
1 teaspoon freshly ground black
   pepper
3 to 4 sprigs fresh oregano
3 to 4 sprigs fresh thyme
1 cup (240 ml) extra-virgin olive oil

This classic is great served on a bed of fava (see page 65) or with Crispy Roasted Potatoes (page 127) or both. Start marinating the octopus the day before you plan to grill it.

1. To prepare the octopus, cut each leg off the hood and cut it into halves or thirds depending on the size of the octopus—thinner parts cook faster. Cut the hood into ½-inch (12-mm) strips. Put all of the octopus in a glass or ceramic container with a lid.

2. In a jar with a lid, combine the honey, salt, and vinegar and stir or shake until the honey is completely dissolved. Add the pepper and pour the mixture over the octopus, then cover and put it in the refrigerator.

3. Cut the oregano and thyme sprigs into halves or thirds, place in a dish, and pour the olive oil over them to thoroughly coat. Leave to infuse for 4 hours.

4. Take the herb sprigs out of the olive oil and layer them over, under, and in between the octopus pieces.

5. Pour the olive oil over the octopus and shake the container a little so it coats the pieces. Put back in the fridge until the next day.

6. Preheat the grill to medium heat with no flames at all; set the grill grate at the highest position from the coals and wait until all your coals have a white coat of ash.

7. While the grill is heating up, drain all the marinade into a pan and bring it to a boil for 30 to 40 seconds, remove from the heat, and let it stand until you are ready to baste.

8. When the coals are ready, put the octopus pieces on the grill with the thinner pieces toward the edges where it is not as hot. If your grill has a lid, close it for about 5 minutes.

9. Take the cover off and baste and turn every piece with the boiled marinade. Keep turning and basting every couple of minutes so all the sides of the octopus get grilled. The thinner pieces need 18 to 20 minutes and the rest about 25 minutes total.

10. When ready, cut into thin slices and serve the octopus with the boiled marinade poured over it.

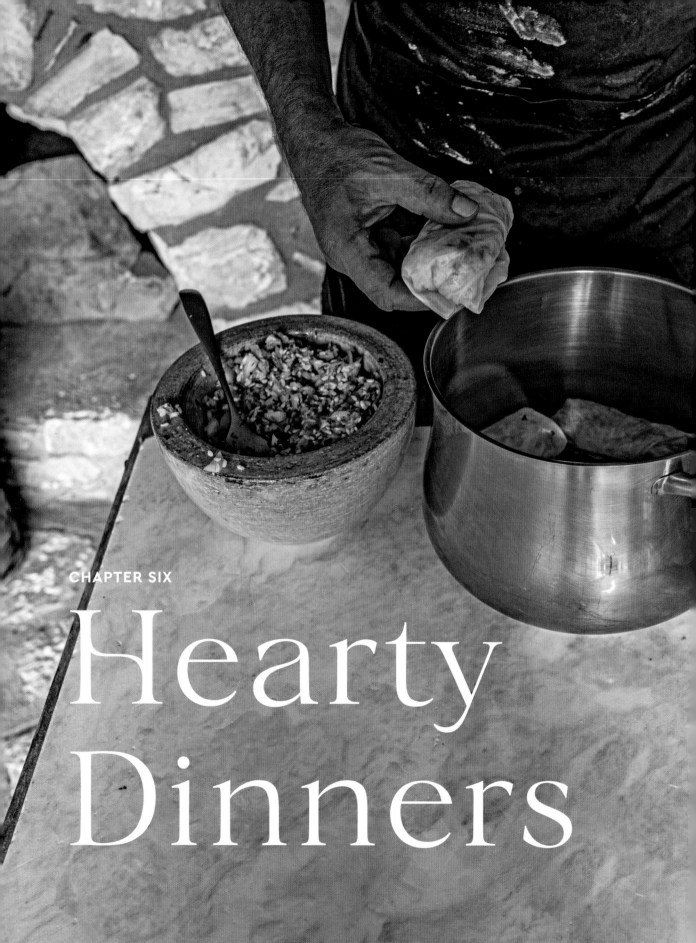

CHAPTER SIX

Hearty Dinners

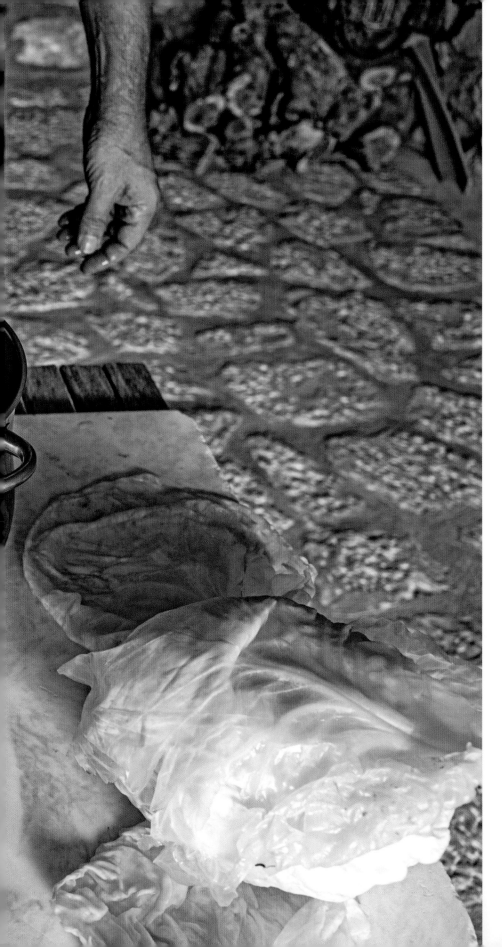

For the Main Meal of the Day and Special Occasions

Βίος ανεόρταστος μακρή (or μακρά) οδός απανδόκευτος.

A life without parties is a long journey without inns.

sunday chickpeas
in the gastra (clay pot)

Serves 6 to 8

Sea salt flakes

1 pound (455 g) dried chickpeas

3 tablespoons baking soda

3 large onions

3 teaspoons freshly ground black pepper

1½ teaspoons berbere spice blend (page 35)

5 bay leaves

Juice and grated zest of 1 lemon (zest optional)

1 cup (240 ml) extra-virgin olive oil

FOR THE DOUGH SEAL

Flour, ideally rye or any kind of wheat flour

The Cycladic island of Sifnos is famous for a dish called revithia sti gastra—chickpeas slow-cooked in a clay dutch oven–like pot called a gastra. Fortunately nowadays you can get gastras on Amazon and other online stores (a dutch oven or a clay pot for baking can also be used). The islanders are passionate about their chickpeas, and almost every family grows their own. They love them so much that they are a regular Sunday treat. They also have a gastra design just for chickpeas that dates back three to four thousand years; its shape is similar to a Spanish bean pot.

The process starts on Friday night, when they place the chickpeas in the gastra, fill it with water, and soak them both. On Saturday evening, they prepare the dish, seal the gastra with dough to make it airtight, and place it in a wood-fired oven until morning. The soaking of the gastra prevents it from absorbing water and creates more steam while in the oven, and the dough seal keeps the steam inside to infuse the chickpeas with all the flavors and keep them moist while they cook slowly overnight. NOTE: The chickpeas need to be soaked 12 to 18 hours in advance.

1. Soak the chickpeas in the gastra full of water with a handful of sea salt flakes for 12 to 18 hours. The chickpeas will double in size.

2. After soaking, drain the water and stir the baking soda into the chickpeas, making sure that it is mixed well and all the chickpeas are coated. This is to soften their skins to make them more digestible. Let sit for another 30 to 60 minutes. Fill the gastra with water, swirl it around and drain; repeat four times.

3. Meanwhile, slice and chop the onions: Cut the center, fatter part of the onions into thin slices, which you are going to layer over the chickpeas, and dice each of the ends, which will be mixed in with the chickpeas.

4. Add the diced onions to the chickpeas, sprinkle with the pepper and most of the berbere, saving a little bit to sprinkle on top at the end. Mix the chickpeas, onions, and spices well.

5. Layer the bay leaves over the chickpeas (be careful not to break the leaves, as you want to remove them whole).

6. Layer the slices of onion on top of everything. Sprinkle on 3 teaspoons sea salt flakes evenly, along with the rest of the berbere. Pour the lemon juice over the top. You can also add some of the lemon zest (about 1 teaspoon), although this is optional. Add the olive oil and 4 cups (960 ml) water. Adding the water last will spread the spices and ingredients throughout the entire pot.

7. Now it's time to seal the pot with dough; this keeps all the steam and juices inside. See the instructions below.

8. For the best results, don't preheat the oven, as it's better to let the pot heat up with the oven. We recommend baking the chickpeas for 6 hours at 350°F (175°C). But there are quicker cooking times if you are in a hurry: 4 hours at 400°F (205°C) or 2½ hours at 425°F (220°C).

9. Remove the gastra from the oven and let it cool for 30 minutes. If the lid is stuck, moisten the seal with a little water, wait for a couple of minutes, and try again.

10. Before you serve, make sure you remove the whole bay leaves.

SEALING THE GASTRA

Mix about equal parts flour and water into a soft Play-Doh–like consistency. For our clay pot we use 3 heaping tablespoons flour to 3 tablespoons water, but this will vary depending on the size of your pot and variety of flour.

Roll it into a long sausage shape ¼ inch (6 mm) wide. Mold it along the open edge of the gastra and then place the lid on top. The dough closes the gap between the pot and its lid, sealing all the moisture and steam in as the pot cooks in the oven. Eventually the steam will gently break the seal and a nice aroma will escape from your oven and into your kitchen, but don't panic: By the time the seal breaks it has worked its wonders.

magiritsa—a four-mushroom chowder

Serves 8

½ cup (120 ml) extra-virgin olive oil

2 teaspoons freshly ground black pepper

2 to 3 cloves garlic, finely chopped or pressed

1½ cups (165 g) chopped onions

2 teaspoons sea salt flakes

2 cups (110 g) chopped scallions (white parts ⅛ inch/3 mm thick, green parts ½ to ¾ inch/12 to 20 mm)

3 cups (720 ml) beer or water

½ cup (95 g) white rice

1 cup (60 g) sliced oyster mushrooms

1 cup (85 g) sliced portobello mushrooms

1 cup (95 g) sliced white button mushrooms

1 cup (95 g) sliced porcini mushrooms (if you can't find fresh, substitute with more oyster, portobello, or white button)

2 heads romaine lettuce, coarsely chopped (about 5 cups/275 g)

¾ cup (40 g) fresh dill, finely chopped

1 tablespoon fresh oregano, finely chopped

4 large eggs

Juice of 1 lemon

A little before midnight strikes on Holy Saturday in Kardamili, its residents switch off their lights and make their way to the main square. There, the priest from the tiny Orthodox church emerges holding a single white candle, and the flame is passed among candles held by the gathered crowd. As the midnight bells ring, fireworks fill the sky and everybody exchanges kisses, then heads home, where magiritsa soup is served.

Traditionally made with sheep's innards, the meal breaks the forty-day Lenten fast. Magiritsa is a favorite of ours. One year we had vegetarian guests, but we didn't want them to miss out on the magiritsa experience. Our mushroom version was born. The rich, earthy, meaty taste of the mushrooms replaces the offal perfectly. A symphony of textures and flavors, this chowder is made with four different kinds of mushrooms, and wilted lettuce; just before serving, eggs mixed with lemon juice are whisked in to enrich the soup.

1. Heat the olive oil in a large pot over high heat. Add the pepper and lower the heat to medium-high.

2. Add the garlic and give it a stir with a wooden spoon. Add the onions and sprinkle the salt over them, let them cook undisturbed for 30 seconds, then mix well and continue to stir for a minute or so until the onions become translucent. Add the scallions. Sauté until the onions soften and turn golden and all the excess liquid in the pan is gone, and you are left only with the oil, about 5 minutes. (If the onions and scallions start sticking to the bottom of the pan, add a little of the beer and scrape the bottom of the pan with your spoon, cooking until most of the beer is gone.)

3. Pour in the rice and toss in the mushrooms. Sauté until everything begins to soften, 5 to 7 minutes. Toss in the lettuce and give it a generous stir. Add the remaining beer. As soon as it starts bubbling, turn the heat to low. Simmer for 30 minutes. Stir in the dill and oregano and keep stirring for 30 seconds; remove from the heat.

4. In a large bowl, beat the eggs well, add the lemon juice, and continue to beat. Take a ladleful of the hot liquid from the pot and mix it a little at a time into the egg-lemon mixture while constantly whisking. Continue to add one ladleful of broth at a time until the temperature of the bowl is hot to the touch. Then pour the egg mixture into the pot and give the soup a thorough stir.

5. Ladle the soup into bowls and serve.

pastitsio with broccoli, zucchini, eggplant, and yogurt béchamel

Serves 12

FOR THE RAGÙ AND PASTA

¼ cup plus 1 tablespoon (75 ml) extra-virgin olive oil, plus more for the baking pan

Sea salt flakes

1 pound (455 g) dried bucatini pasta (or long ziti or penne)

1 teaspoon freshly ground black pepper

1 tablespoon minced garlic

2 cups (180 g) minced onions

2 teaspoons berbere spice mix (page 35)

1 cup (80 g) diced eggplant (½-inch/12-mm cubes)

1½ cups (170 g) sliced zucchini (¼-inch/6-mm slices)

1½ cups (125 g) sliced white button or oyster mushrooms

1½ cups (360 ml) beer

1½ cups (135 g) small broccoli florets

Pastitsio is a baked layered pasta dish. On the bottom is a layer of bucatini, in the middle a layer of ragù alla bolognese, and the whole thing is topped with a layer of béchamel sauce. This one is made with a meatless, tomato-less broccoli, zucchini, mushroom, and eggplant ragù and topped with our yogurt and cheese béchamel sauce. (For a more traditional pastitsio featuring beef, see page 213.)

1. Preheat the oven to 350°F (175°C). Lightly oil a 13 × 9 × 2-inch (33 × 12 × 6-cm) baking pan.

2. Make the pasta and ragù: Bring a large pot of salted water to a boil, add the 1 tablespoon olive oil and the pasta, and cook according to the package instructions minus 30 to 45 seconds. When the pasta is ready, drain and set aside.

3. Meanwhile, heat ¼ cup (60 ml) of the olive oil in a large skillet over high heat. Add the pepper and lower the heat to medium-high. Add the garlic and give it a stir with a wooden spoon, then add the onions and sprinkle 2 teaspoons salt over them. Cook without disturbing for 30 seconds, then add the berbere, mix well, and sauté until the onions wilt and turn golden brown, all the excess liquid in the pan evaporates, and they are left only with the oil, 5 to 7 minutes. Add the eggplant, zucchini, and mushrooms and sauté until the eggplant turns from white to a semi-transparent color, 5 to 7 minutes. Add the beer and stir. As soon as it starts bubbling, turn the heat to low.

4. Simmer for 20 to 30 minutes, until all the liquid is gone and all that is left is the oil and vegetables. Add the broccoli, parsley, and oregano and keep stirring for 30 seconds. Remove from the heat and set the ragù aside.

1 cup (50 g) finely chopped fresh
    parsley

1 teaspoon dried oregano

2 large eggs

½ cup (50 g) grated parmesan
    cheese

FOR THE YOGURT BÉCHAMEL

4 large eggs

4 cups (960 ml) whole milk Greek
    yogurt

2 cups (300 g) crumbled feta
    cheese

2 cups (240 to 250 g) crumbled
    fresh mizithra cheese
    (or manouri or ricotta)

¾ cup (70 g) grated aged mizithra
    cheese (or parmesan)

2 tablespoons bread crumbs

5. In the baking pan, spread the cooked pasta in a layer 1 inch (2.5 cm) deep at the most. Save any remaining pasta for another use.

6. In a small mixing bowl, beat the eggs, then add the cheese, mix well, and pour over the pasta while tossing so it coats all of the pasta. Spread into an even layer.

7. Make the yogurt béchamel: In a large mixing bowl, combine the eggs and the yogurt, feta, fresh mizithra, and all but 3 tablespoons of the aged mizithra; blend thoroughly using an immersion blender until it becomes smooth and creamy.

8. Take 1 cup (240 ml) of the yogurt béchamel and mix it well with the vegetable ragù, then scoop the ragù over the pasta and spread it in an even layer.

9. Pour the remaining yogurt béchamel over the top and spread it evenly. Sprinkle the top with the reserved mizithra and the bread crumbs.

10. Bake for 30 to 40 minutes, until the top starts to turn golden brown. Remove from the oven and let it cool for 15 to 20 minutes before cutting and serving warm.

TIP: You can make this pastitsio a day in advance. After it cools completely, cover and put in the refrigerator. Take it out of the fridge about 1½ hours before reheating. Preheat the oven to 300°F (150°C). Heat the pastitsio for 15 to 20 minutes.

pastitsio with lentils, vegetables, and yogurt béchamel

Serves 12

FOR THE RAGÙ AND PASTA

1 cup (190 g) brown lentils (red, green, or yellow work too)

Sea salt flakes

¼ cup plus 1 tablespoon (75 ml) extra-virgin olive oil, plus more for the baking pan

1 pound (455 g) dried bucatini pasta (or long ziti or penne)

2 teaspoons freshly ground black pepper

1 tablespoon chopped garlic

2 cups (180 g) diced onions

3 teaspoons ground cumin

1 teaspoon chili powder

1 cup (80 g) cubed eggplant (½- to ¾-inch/12- to 20-mm cubes)

1 cup (110 g) shredded carrots

¾ cup (180 ml) pale ale

2 cups (150 g) blanched and peeled ripe tomatoes (or canned)

¾ cup (40 g) chopped fresh parsley

1 teaspoon dried oregano

In this pastitsio, tender lentils take the place of ground beef, and you'll never miss the meat. Be sure to plan ahead and soak the lentils overnight so they cook evenly.

1. In a bowl, soak the lentils overnight in water to cover. Drain and rinse.

2. Make the pasta and ragù: Bring a pot of salted water to a boil, add the 1 tablespoon oil and the pasta, and cook according to the package instructions minus 30 to 45 seconds. When the pasta is ready, drain and set aside.

3. Meanwhile, heat ¼ cup (60 ml) of the olive oil in a large skillet over high heat. Add the pepper and lower the heat to medium-high. Add the garlic and give it a stir with a wooden spoon, then add the onions and sprinkle 2 teaspoons salt over them; cook without disturbing for 30 seconds. Add the cumin and chili powder, mix well, and sauté until the onions wilt and turn golden brown, all the excess liquid in the pan evaporates, and they are left only with the olive oil, 5 to 7 minutes.

4. Add the lentils, eggplant, and carrots and sauté for another 6 minutes. If the lentils start to stick, pour in a drop of the beer and stir. Add the tomatoes. Slowly pour all of the beer into the pot, stirring gently as you go. Once the liquid begins to boil, lower the heat to a gentle simmer.

5. Simmer until all the excess liquid is gone and all that is left is the oil, 20 to 30 minutes. Stir in the parsley and oregano and keep stirring for 30 seconds. Remove from the heat and set the ragù aside.

6. While the ragù is simmering, preheat the oven to 350°F (175°C). Lightly oil a 13 × 9 × 2-inch (33 × 12 × 6-cm) baking pan.

FOR THE YOGURT BÉCHAMEL

4 large medium eggs

4 cups (960 ml) whole milk Greek yogurt

2 cups (300 g) crumbled feta cheese

2 cups (240 to 250 g) crumbled fresh mizithra cheese (or manouri or ricotta)

¾ cup (70 g) grated aged mizithra cheese (or parmesan)

2 tablespoons bread crumbs

7. In the baking pan, spread the cooked pasta in a layer 1 inch (2.5 cm) deep at the most. Save any remaining pasta for another use.

8. Make the yogurt béchamel: In a large mixing bowl, combine the eggs and the yogurt, feta, fresh mizithra, and all but 3 tablespoons of the aged mizithra; blend thoroughly using an immersion blender until it becomes smooth and creamy.

9. Take 1 cup (240 ml) of the yogurt béchamel and mix it well with the vegetable ragù, then scoop the ragù over the pasta and spread it in an even layer.

10. Pour the remaining yogurt béchamel over the top and spread it evenly. Sprinkle the top with the reserved mizithra cheese and the bread crumbs.

11. Bake for 30 to 40 minutes, until the top starts to turn golden brown. Remove from the oven and let it cool for 15 to 20 minutes before cutting and serving warm.

TIP: You can make this pastitsio a day in advance. After it cools completely, cover and put in the refrigerator. Take it out of the fridge about 1½ hours before reheating. Preheat the oven to 300°F (150°C). Heat the pastitsio for 15 to 20 minutes.

gemista—stuffed peppers with turkey, quinoa, spinach, and mushrooms

Serves 4 to 6

1 cup (170 g) quinoa

4 teaspoons sea salt flakes

½ cup (120 ml) extra-virgin olive oil, plus more for the quinoa, the peppers, and the baking dish

4 teaspoons berbere spice blend (see page 35)

2½ teaspoons ground cumin

½ teaspoon chili powder or ground cayenne pepper, plus more to taste

1½ to 2 cups (145 g) chopped cremini or button mushrooms

8 cups (240 g) fresh spinach, or 1 (10-ounce/280-g) box frozen spinach, defrosted and squeezed dry

½ teaspoon freshly ground black pepper

1 pound (455 g) ground turkey

2 to 3 cloves garlic, pressed

2 medium onions, diced

8 bell peppers (2 each of red, orange, yellow, and green) with flat bottoms

Peppers are not native to Greece; they arrived from the New World in the late fifteenth century, and now they are ubiquitous in Mediterranean cuisine. Our gemista nods to the pepper's origin by substituting quinoa for rice and using turkey instead of beef, giving a uniquely American twist to the traditional stuffed pepper. The berbere spice blend gives the filling a complex depth of flavor, and the chili powder gives it an extra kick. This version has officially replaced the more traditional one in our household. Serve these with a simple green salad.

Be sure to choose peppers that have a flat enough bottom that they can stand upright in the baking dish.

1. Cook the quinoa in water following the package instructions, adding 1 teaspoon salt and a splash of olive oil to the boiling water. Set aside.

2. Coat the bottom of a sauté pan with about ¼ cup (60 ml) of the olive oil and add 2 teaspoons of the berbere, 1 teaspoon of the cumin, and ¼ teaspoon of the chili powder. Place over high heat.

3. Add the mushrooms and spinach to the pan and stir. Cover the pan; this helps the spinach cook faster. Once the spinach starts to wilt, stir in 1 teaspoon salt. Cook until the mushrooms are soft and the spinach has wilted completely, about 10 minutes. Transfer to a bowl.

4. To the pan, add the remaining ¼ cup (60 ml) of olive oil, the remaining 2 teaspoons berbere, 1½ teaspoons cumin, ¼ teaspoon chili powder, and the black pepper.

5. Add the turkey and cook, stirring continuously, to brown the meat and break up any large pieces. While you are stirring, add 1½ teaspoons salt. Once the meat has browned, stir in the garlic and cook until fragrant, about 2 minutes.

6. Add the onions, sprinkle the remaining ½ teaspoon salt over them, and let cook undisturbed for 30 seconds. Stir well and cook until translucent, 2 to 5 minutes.

7. Preheat the oven to 400°F (205°C). Coat the bottom of a 13 × 9 × 2-inch (33 × 12 × 6-cm) baking dish with olive oil.

8. Stir the quinoa and the mushroom mixture into the turkey mixture and turn off the heat but let the pan sit on the warm burner.

9. Cut the tops off the peppers but do not discard them. Remove all the seeds from the inside of the peppers and any that may be on the tops. Fill and pack the hollowed peppers with the turkey mixture, cover the peppers with their tops, and stand them upright in the prepared baking dish.

10. Use a pastry brush to coat the outsides of the peppers with olive oil, including the tops. Bake for 1 hour 15 minutes, or until the peppers have softened and the tops have started to brown. Let cool slightly and serve warm.

traditional beef dolmades

Serves 4

FOR THE DOLMADES

1 large head of green cabbage or
romaine lettuce, separated
into leaves

2 medium onions

¾ pound (310 g) ground beef

1¼ cups (238 g) any long-grain
white rice

2½ cups (125 g) finely chopped
fresh parsley

2½ cups (125 g) finely chopped
fresh dill

2 to 3 tablespoons extra-virgin
olive oil

1 tablespoon sea salt flakes

1 teaspoon freshly ground black
pepper, plus more to taste

FOR THE EGG-LEMON SAUCE

2 large eggs

Juice of ½ lemon

1 tablespoon cornstarch

Beef dolmades can be made with a variety of leaves as wrapping; the most common is cabbage, but we also love lettuce (as shown, page 192).

One time during a visit from my yiayia (grandmother), she and Dad decided to make dolmades together. They chopped and prepped all the ingredients, working in perfect harmony—until it came time to wrap the dolma. A brawl broke out. My dad wanted to use lettuce, and Yiayia didn't want to hear it. "Are you crazy? We don't make dolmades with lettuce!" Dad suggested they roll half with cabbage and half with lettuce. She was not happy at all, but she gave in, grumbling the whole time about Dad's cooking habits and how he wasn't following tradition. Then as my dad was lifting her dolmades to join his in the cooking pot, she let out a shriek. "No way are you gonna spoil my perfect dolmades," Yiayia said. "Cook yours separately." Dad had no choice but to submit this time, and they cooked them in two pots.

We sat down to eat, and for a long time Yiayia refused to try the lettuce variety. But she couldn't resist, so she grabbed one on the sly, saying she'd just have one bite. After a prolonged *mmmm*, she ate the rest of it and said, "What do you know. They are good. Different, but not bad." —OLIVIA

1. Wash the cabbage leaves, then blanch them by dipping them in boiling water for 45 to 60 seconds. Set aside.

2. Using the largest holes on a box grater, grate the onions. In a bowl, combine the onions, beef, rice, parsley, dill, olive oil, salt, and pepper and mix by hand.

3. Scoop 1 tablespoon of the mixture onto the large part of a cabbage leaf—the raised cabbage vein should be on the inside of the roll—and roll for a few turns before folding in the sides. Continue rolling all the way up to the end and set aside. Repeat with the remaining filling and leaves.

4. Line the base of a small round pot with the dolmades, covering the surface and then stacking them in layers. Pour in 2 cups (480 ml) water, bring to a boil, then lower the heat and gently simmer for 40 minutes. It's a good idea to place a heavy plate on top of the dolmades as they cook, to keep them in place.

5. Meanwhile, make the egg-lemon sauce: In a bowl, beat the eggs, adding the lemon juice and cornstarch.

6. When the dolmades are cooked, ladle some of the hot liquid from the pot into the egg mixture in small amounts, stirring constantly (add the liquid until the bowl feels hot to the touch). Pour the sauce over the dolmades and serve.

roast chicken with lemon and herbs

Serves 4

¾ cup (180 ml) extra-virgin olive oil
1 whole 3- to 4-pound (1.3- to
    1.8-kg) chicken
2 medium onions, 1 quartered,
    1 sliced
2 lemons, halved
4 to 5 potatoes, peeled and
    quartered
1 tablespoon dried oregano
1½ teaspoons dried thyme
1½ teaspoons dried rosemary
½ to 1 teaspoon sea salt flakes
½ to 1 teaspoon freshly ground
    black pepper

A classic: simple and always delicious. The onion and lemon inside the chicken keep it moist during cooking, so this roast chicken is always juicy.

1. Preheat the oven to 375°F (190°C). Coat the bottom of a roasting pan with about ¼ cup (60 ml) olive oil.

2. Remove any innards from the chicken and reserve for another use or discard. Place the chicken in the center of the roasting pan and stuff it with a quartered onion and a lemon half. Then alternate with the remaining onion quarters and lemon halves, or as many as will fit. Leftover onion quarters can roast with the chicken; leftover lemons can be squeezed over the bird before it goes into the oven.

3. Place the potatoes, followed by the sliced onion, around the chicken.

4. Drizzle olive oil on top of the chicken (about ¼ cup/60 ml) and on top of the potatoes and onions (about ¼ cup/60 ml).

5. Squeeze the juice of the remaining lemon on top of the contents of the pan.

6. Sprinkle the oregano, thyme, rosemary, salt, and pepper over the chicken, potatoes, and onion.

7. Bake for 1 hour 25 minutes to 1 hour 40 minutes, depending on the size of the chicken. The top of the chicken should be a toasty, golden brown and the juices should be clear rather than pink when the thigh joint is pierced with a small knife. Serve and enjoy.

berbere spiced chicken

Serves 4

1½ pounds (680 g) boneless, skinless chicken thighs (about 8)

½ cup (120 ml) extra-virgin olive oil

1 teaspoon freshly ground black pepper

2 teaspoons berbere spice blend (page 35)

2 cups (220 g) chopped onions

1 tablespoon crushed garlic

2 teaspoons sea salt flakes

1 cup (240 ml) lager, plus more if needed (you don't need to use an expensive one)

Cooked rice, for serving

Dad and I discovered berbere in Rome while sitting in a café near the Campo de' Fiori market. "Something smells really good," Dad said, before following his nose like a bloodhound to the spice stand. There, the seller told him about a chile-spice blend called berbere, an essential addition to Ethiopian dishes from vegetables to meats and stews. After that day, it has earned a permanent place on our kitchen shelves and in our hearts and has also become a favorite among our friends. We now mix our own berbere using black cardamom, kings cumin (also known as ajowan or carom), fenugreek, and paprika, to name a few ingredients.

—OLIVIA

1. Cut each chicken thigh in half and set aside.

2. Heat the olive oil in a large skillet over high heat. Add the pepper and lower the heat to medium-high.

3. Place the chicken pieces in the pan and cook until browned. Stir for a few minutes, then add the berbere. Stir again and follow with the onions and garlic. When the onions are lightly golden, add the salt and stir well.

4. Slowly pour in the lager, stir, and when the liquid starts to boil, lower the heat to medium. Cook until the lager has completely reduced, at least 20 minutes. If it becomes too dry before the 20 minutes have passed and the contents begin to stick to the pan, add a little more lager. Serve hot with rice.

EMBRACING THE UNKNOWN

When I was young and visiting Greece with my family, food was always an adventure: I never knew what the dish was or what I was about to eat. I loved, but was also a little horrified, hearing how my papou's favorite parts of spit-roasted lamb were the brain and the eyeballs.

But gradually, with the help of my dad, I learned to appreciate unfamiliar foods. For a long time I claimed that I hated and wouldn't eat onions, for example. Dad, rather than trying to persuade me to give them another try, used them as a base for a delicious chicken and tomato sauce, which he served over rice. I devoured plates of it and declared that it was my new favorite meal. So, when my dad broke the news that I had just eaten onions, the argument was over before it had even started. Twenty years later, I'm still making that dish—and adding sautéed onions and garlic to just about everything.

Dad taught Livi and me to be open-minded and adventurous, even if he sometimes resorted to creative means to do so. Today I'm grateful, and I've learned to apply his attitudes not only to food but also to life.

—CHLOE

chicken thighs in tomato sauce over rice

Serves 4

¼ cup (60 ml) extra-virgin olive oil

½ teaspoon freshly ground black pepper, plus more to taste

3 cloves garlic, minced

1 large or 2 small onions, chopped

1 teaspoon cumin

1½ pounds (680 g) boneless, skinless chicken thighs (about 8)

2 teaspoons sea salt flakes, plus more to taste

1 (6-ounce/170-g) can tomato paste

1 (6-ounce/180-ml) can V8 juice

½ bottle lager

Cooked white rice

Grated parmesan cheese (optional)

This was arguably Chloe's favorite dish growing up, as well as the confirmation that Dad had won the onion debate. The serving size says 4, but if you invite Chloe, then possibly only 2 or 3.   —OLIVIA

1. Heat the olive oil in a large skillet over high heat. Add the pepper and lower the heat to medium-high.

2. Add the garlic and cook until fragrant, 2 minutes. Toss in the onions and cumin and cook until the onions turn golden, 5 to 8 minutes.

3. Add the chicken to the pan, sprinkle with a pinch each of salt and pepper on each side, and cook until browned.

4. Add the tomato paste and stir for a minute, then add the V8 juice, 2 cans full of water, and the lager and bring to a boil. Turn the heat to low and allow the mixture to simmer. Cook until the sauce has thickened enough so if you scrape the bottom of the pan it takes a few seconds for the gap to close, 20 to 25 minutes.

5. Add more salt and pepper to taste. Serve over white rice and with parmesan cheese if desired.

hot honey-orange chicken

Serves 4

4 boneless, skinless chicken
   breasts (1½ to 2 pounds/
   680 to 900 g), cut into 1½-inch
   (4-cm) strips
1 batch Fresh Honey-Orange
   Marmalade (page 250)
3 tablespoons minced fresh ginger
3 cloves garlic, pressed
½ cup (120 ml) soy sauce
½ to 1 teaspoon berbere spice
   blend (page 35), depending on
   how spicy your berbere is
1 teaspoon sesame seeds
Cooked rice for serving

Growing up, one of our favorite dishes our mom made was "sticky chicky," a chicken wing dish very similar to this one with orange marmalade and soy sauce. As you can guess, sticky fingers followed every bite. This rendition is healthier and a little less messy!

—OLIVIA

1. In a bowl, combine the chicken strips, marmalade, ginger, garlic, soy sauce, and berbere. Mix it well and let it marinate in the refrigerator for 45 minutes to 1 hour.

2. Preheat the oven to 375°F (190°C).

3. Put the chicken and marinade in a baking dish (try to have a single layer of chicken), and pour any extra marinade on top. Sprinkle some of the sesame seeds on top. Bake for 15 minutes, then flip the chicken to bake on the other side. Cook for another 15 to 20 minutes, turning the oven temperature up to 450°F (230°C) for the last 5 minutes to help thicken the sauce and make it a little more golden in color.

4. Sprinkle more sesame seeds on top, serve over rice, and enjoy!

chicken thighs with sliced ginger, honey, lime, and cilantro

Serves 4

1½ pounds (680 g) boneless, skinless chicken thighs (about 8)

2 tablespoons sliced fresh ginger

1 tablespoon honey

2 limes

½ cup (20 g) chopped fresh cilantro, plus 1 cup (40 g) for serving, if you'd like

2 cloves garlic

½ cup (120 ml) extra-virgin olive oil, plus 2 tablespoons for cooking

1 small onion, sliced

2 to 3 scallions, chopped (white parts ⅛ inch/3 mm thick, green parts ½ to ¾ inch/12 to 20 mm)

Sea salt flakes and freshly ground black pepper

Cooked rice, for serving

This versatile chicken dish can be devoured in numerous ways. It's perfect as the main course for dinner with just about any vegetable as the side. Chloe's favorite way is to make it "Grexican" and have it over rice in a bowl with feta cheese, extra cilantro, avocado, and a fruity salsa. Our Orange Pico de Gallo (page 63) is always a fantastic option.

1. In a bowl, marinate the chicken in the ginger, honey, the juice of one of the limes, the ½ cup (20 g) cilantro, the garlic, and ¼ cup (60 ml) oil for at least 1 hour in the refrigerator or up to overnight.

2. Heat a skillet on high with ¼ cup (60 ml) of the olive oil and add the onion and scallions; cook for 5 minutes. Add the chicken with all the marinade and stir into the onion. Allow the chicken to brown, cooking for 5 to 8 minutes per side, then lower the heat to medium and cover. Continue cooking for 20 minutes, or until a meat thermometer reads 356°F (180°C).

3. Remove from the heat. Squeeze the second lime over the cooked chicken and season with salt and pepper to taste. If you'd like, toss extra fresh cilantro into the dish just before serving over rice.

homemade chicken tenders with sea salt and honey hot sauce #3

Serves 4

²/₃ cup (65 g) dry bread crumbs
⅓ cup (45 g) cornstarch
⅓ cup (40 g) all-purpose flour
3 large eggs
½ cup plus 2 tablespoons (150 ml)
    extra-virgin olive oil
1 clove garlic, pressed
½ teaspoon sea salt flakes
½ teaspoon freshly ground black
    pepper
4 boneless, skinless chicken
    breasts (1½ to 2 pounds/
    680 to 900 g), cut into
    1½-inch (4-cm) strips
4 tablespoons (60 ml) Sea Salt and
    Honey Hot Sauce #3 (page 67)
Gorgonzola Greek Yogurt Dip
    (page 68)

Baked chicken strips with a crunchy coating (the secret is the olive oil in the dredging), doused in a honeyed hot sauce and dunked into a creamy gorgonzola dip, is one of our odes to American buffalo wings. (See the cauliflower version on page 45 for another.) Serve with cold, refreshing celery sticks and plenty of napkins—or forks, for fancier occasions.

1. Preheat the oven to 475°F (245°C) and position a rack in the top third of the oven. Line a rimmed baking sheet with parchment paper.

2. On a plate, mix the bread crumbs, cornstarch, and flour together well and spread it out. Set aside. (We sometimes use a sheet of aluminum foil instead of a plate to make cleanup easier.)

3. In a bowl, combine the eggs, ½ cup (120 ml) of the olive oil, the garlic, salt, and pepper, beating to mix well.

4. Submerge the chicken strips in the egg mixture, then toss them in the flour mixture until fully coated; shake off any excess flour and lay the chicken on the baking sheet.

5. Once all the chicken is on the baking sheet, spoon the excess egg mixture onto the chicken strips.

6. Bake in the top third of the oven (this helps the chicken strips become crispier) for 10 minutes, then flip the chicken onto the other side. Continue baking for another 5 minutes.

7. Remove from the oven and cut into the largest strip to see if it's cooked all the way through; if not, put back in the oven and cook for another 2 to 3 minutes. (After 18 minutes of cooking, the chicken should be done.)

8. In a bowl, combine the hot sauce and 2 tablespoons oil. Mix well. Toss the chicken in the mixture until lightly coated with sauce. Serve immediately while hot and enjoy with the dip.

TIP: You can skip the hot sauce step for healthy, crowd-pleasing chicken tenders!

DON'T BE AFRAID TO EXPERIMENT

Nicholas: The owner of a bar at Kalogria beach told me about how he infuses bottles of raki with cucumber peels for a refreshing change of pace in summertime. I thought that sounded like a good idea, so I went out in the garden and picked a cucumber. I put the peels in a jar and covered them with raki. I sliced some of the cucumber and had a nice salad for myself. But I had more than half a cucumber left—and always had more raki, of course—so I diced that, too, and covered it with liquor and put it aside on the counter.

That evening I was hosting a dinner party and people were hungry before the meal was ready, so I put the liquor-soaked cucumber cubes in a bowl with little toothpicks. A very classy hors d'oeuvre, I thought—

Dimitri: It was an explosion of fire in my mouth that burned and made my eyes water.

Nicholas: Maybe if I'd served them chilled—

Olivia: No.

Nicholas: Well, some of us liked it.

chicken in the gastra with leeks, mushrooms, and tarragon

Serves 4

7 to 8 sprigs fresh tarragon
1 whole (3- to 4-pound) chicken that will fit in your gastra with the lid on
2 teaspoons sea salt flakes
2 teaspoons freshly ground black pepper
1 lemon, quartered
1 cup (95 g) sliced mushrooms
3 leeks, sliced and washed well
¼ cup (60 ml) extra-virgin olive oil

This method for baking a whole chicken in a clay gastra leaves you with the best of both worlds: juicy, tarragon-scented chicken with crisp, bronzed skin.

1. Put 4 or 5 tarragon sprigs in a gastra and pour in ¾ cup (180 ml) water.

2. Lift the chicken skin and stuff a couple of tarragon sprigs underneath.

3. Season the chicken with salt and pepper (use about half the salt and pepper) inside and out, stuff the rest of the tarragon and the lemon pieces in the chicken cavity, and lay it on top of the tarragon bed in the gastra.

4. In a bowl, toss the mushrooms and leeks with the remaining salt and pepper and put them in the gastra around the chicken.

5. Pour the olive oil over everything.

6. Cover the gastra, put it in a cold oven, and turn the oven to 375°F (190°C). Bake for 1½ hours. Take the lid off and bake for 15 to 20 minutes to get a nice crispy golden-brown skin.

7. Transfer the chicken and vegetables from the gastra to a serving plate.

8. Drain all the liquid from the gastra into a frying pan (using a spoon to remove any excess fat from the top, if you'd like) bring it to a boil, and cook for a few minutes to reduce it, then pour into a gravy bowl to serve alongside the chicken and vegetables.

chicken livers with scallions, cilantro, and cumin

Serves 4

¼ cup (60 ml) extra-virgin olive oil

½ teaspoon freshly ground black pepper, plus more if needed

1 pound (455 g) chicken livers

2 cloves garlic, minced

6 to 8 scallions, chopped (white part ⅛ inch/3 mm thick; green part ½ to ¾ inch/12 to 20 mm)

2 teaspoons sea salt flakes

1 teaspoon ground cumin

½ cup (120 ml) white wine

Juice of 1 lime

½ teaspoon dried oregano

Handful of fresh cilantro

Cumin and cilantro may not be traditional ingredients with chicken livers, and you might have to explain yourself to guests who aren't expecting them, but why not try it? They complement and brighten the minerally chicken liver flavor nicely. Serve with Spicy and Crisp Oven-Baked Piri-Piri Fries (page 41 and shown opposite), Crispy Roasted Potatoes (page 127), mashed potatoes, or saffron rice. If you have any leftovers you can puree them to make chicken liver pâté.

1. In a large saucepan, heat the olive oil over high heat. Add the pepper and lower the heat to medium-high. Add the livers and cook, stirring with a wooden spoon, until they turn light in color and then start turning brown. Stir in the garlic and cook until fragrant, about 1 minute.

2. Add the scallions, sprinkle 2 teaspoons salt over them, and let cook undisturbed for 30 seconds. Add the cumin. Mix well and continue to stir until the scallions begin to change from white to translucent, 1 minute or so, then add the wine. Sauté until all the wine is evaporated and the livers are brown outside and pink but not bloody inside.

3. Add the lime juice, oregano, and cilantro and cook for an additional 1 minute. Serve.

chicken livers in a rich tomato sauce

Serves 4 to 6

¼ cup (60 ml) extra-virgin olive oil
½ teaspoon freshly ground black
    pepper, plus more to taste
1 pound (455 g) chicken livers
½ bottle lager
2 cloves garlic, minced
2 onions, chopped
2 teaspoons sea salt flakes, plus
    more to taste
1 teaspoon ground cumin
1 (6-ounce/170-g) can tomato
    paste
1 (8-ounce/240-ml) can V8 juice
2 teaspoons dried oregano
Handful of fresh cilantro
Cooked white rice

In the summer after second grade I went to camp for a month. Our first dinner there, this dish was served, and I remember everyone had seconds and thirds until there was no more and they had to make omelets for the staff because we'd eaten all the food. This dish, served over rice, remains one of my all-time favorites—the ultimate comfort food.

—NICHOLAS

1. Heat the olive oil in a large saucepan over high heat. Add the pepper and lower the heat to medium-high. Add the livers and cook, stirring with a wooden spoon, until they turn light in color and then start turning brown. If they start to stick to the bottom of the pan, pour in a splash of the beer and mix well, scraping the bottom of the pan, and cook until there is no more liquid in the saucepan. Stir in the garlic and cook until fragrant, about 1 minute.

2. Add the onions, sprinkle 2 teaspoons salt over them, and let cook undisturbed for 30 seconds. Add the cumin. Mix well and continue to stir until the onions become translucent and golden, about 5 minutes. If the ingredients start to stick to the bottom of the pan, add another splash of beer.

3. Mix in the tomato paste, stir well for 1 minute, then add the V8 juice and stir. Bring to a boil, then turn the heat to low. Simmer for 30 to 40 minutes, stirring occasionally, until you can drag the spoon along the bottom of the pan and there is no excess liquid and the sauce is slow to close the gap.

4. Taste for salt and pepper and add more if needed, stir well. Add the oregano and cilantro and cook for an additional 1 to 2 minutes. Serve with rice.

pastitsio with beef, eggplant, and yogurt béchamel

Serves 12

FOR THE RAGÙ AND PASTA

1 pound (455 g) eggplant

3 teaspoons sea salt flakes, plus
    more for the pasta water

6 tablespoons (90 ml) extra-virgin
    olive oil, plus more for the pan

1 teaspoon freshly ground black
    pepper

1 pound (455 g) ground beef

2 cups (220 g) diced onions

1 tablespoon minced garlic

1 teaspoon berbere spice blend
    (page 35)

1 (12-ounce/330-ml) bottle lager

2 cups (450 g) peeled, diced fresh
    tomatoes or 1 (14.5-ounce/411-g)
    can diced tomatoes

½ cup (120 ml) tomato puree

1 cup (50 g) fresh parsley, chopped

1 pound (455 g) dried bucatini
    pasta (or penne rigate)

Pastitsio is the ultimate dish for sharing with guests. We usually make this on weekends, when dinners can last until the wee hours of morning. We invite friends, serve with a salad, and dig in. Our yogurt béchamel was born from trying to find an alternative to a traditional béchamel sauce, which uses flour and butter. We buy manouri from a local farmer a few villages north of Kardamili. A creamy, soft goat's milk cheese, it can be difficult to source, but ricotta would make a decent substitute. We also make vegetarian versions of this dish (pages 183 and 186), which friends in the village still rave about!

1. Make the ragù and pasta: Remove the stalk from the eggplant, but leave the skin on. Cut into small cubes and place on a flat dish. Sprinkle 1 teaspoon salt over them, then cover with another plate and weigh that down with something heavy. Leave for 1 hour. This drains the eggplant of its high water content and takes away some of the bitterness.

2. Just before the eggplant is ready, heat a large pan over high heat and add 2½ tablespoons of the olive oil and the pepper. Add the beef and cook until browned. Remove the beef from the pan and set aside in a bowl. In the same pan, sauté the onions and garlic with the remaining 2 teaspoons salt in another 2½ tablespoons of olive oil until golden brown.

3. Squeeze and drain the eggplant and add it to the onions along with the browned beef and the berbere. When the eggplant turns from white to a semitransparent color, add a small amount of the lager and stir.

4. Add the tomatoes and tomato puree and give it another stir. Once the sauce begins to boil, add the rest of the lager and lower the heat. Simmer until all the excess liquid has evaporated and you have a thick, chunky sauce, 20 to 30 minutes. Just before it is cooked, add the parsley.

FOR THE YOGURT BÉCHAMEL

4 large eggs

4 cups (960 ml) whole milk Greek
    yogurt

2 cups (300 g) crumbled feta
    cheese

2 cups (240 to 250 g) crumbled
    fresh mizithra cheese
    (or manouri or ricotta)

¾ cup (70 g) grated aged mizithra
    cheese (or parmesan)

2 tablespoons dried bread crumbs

5. Meanwhile, bring a pot of salted water to a boil, add the remaining 1 tablespoon olive oil and the pasta, and cook according to the package instructions minus 30 to 45 seconds. When the pasta is ready, drain and set aside.

6. While the ragù is simmering and the pasta is cooking, preheat the oven to 350°F (175°C). Lightly oil a 13 × 9 × 2-inch (33 × 12 × 6-cm) baking pan.

7. Make the yogurt béchamel: In a large bowl, combine the eggs, yogurt, feta, and fresh mizithra and mix thoroughly using an immersion blender until you have a smooth cream.

8. Put the bucatini in the prepared baking pan and sprinkle in half of the aged mizithra. Mix together and make an even layer of the pasta on the bottom. Spoon the beef and eggplant sauce over the pasta. Finally, pour the yogurt béchamel over the top and dust with the rest of the aged mizithra and the bread crumbs.

9. Bake for 30 to 40 minutes, until the top turns golden brown. Remove from the oven and let it stand and cool for 15 to 20 minutes before cutting and serving warm.

sofia's lemonato beef

Serves 4

2 teaspoons sea salt flakes
2 teaspoons freshly ground black
   pepper
9 to 12 slivers of garlic (3 to
   4 cloves garlic, cut lengthwise)
1 (3 pound/1.4 kg) boneless beef
   rump roast, tied
¼ cup (120 ml) extra-virgin olive
   oil, plus more for brushing the
   meat
1 cup (240 ml) warm water
Juice of 2 lemons

In this crowd-pleasing classic, a beef roast is slowly braised on the stovetop until tender, then doused with fresh lemon juice. The resulting pan sauce is perfect just as it is—no need to add flour or other thickeners.

1. In a small bowl, mix the salt, pepper, and garlic.

2. Pat the roast dry with paper towels. Use the tip of a sharp knife to make 9 to 12 small incisions all over the roast and put a sliver of garlic into each cut. Brush with olive oil and rub the salt and pepper on it. Allow the beef to stand, covered, at room temperature, for 1½ to 2 hours.

3. In a large, deep pot or dutch oven, heat ¼ cup (60 ml) of the olive oil over high heat. Carefully place the beef in the pot. Using a long fork, start slowly turning the beef so it browns on all sides. When the beef is browned all over, lower the heat to medium-low and carefully pour in the warm water (it will splatter); cover and simmer for 1½ to 2 hours, turning the roast every 10 to 15 minutes, until the internal temperature of the beef is 145 to 150°F (63 to 65°C). If no liquid remains and the beef is not done, add ½ cup (120 ml) warm water at a time until the beef is fully cooked.

4. When the beef is done, turn the heat to high and cook to evaporate any excess water that is left so only olive oil and meat juices remain in the pot. Add the lemon juice and cook for a couple of minutes more, turning on every side.

5. Let the beef cool for 10 to 15 minutes, then slice and serve with the gravy from the pot (use the gravy as is; do not add water or flour).

beef liver on the grill

Serves 2

7 to 8 sprigs fresh thyme
7 to 8 sprigs fresh oregano
2 to 3 cups (480 to 720 ml)
    buttermilk
2 slices (200 g) beef liver
2 teaspoons freshly ground black
    pepper
½ cup (120 ml) extra-virgin olive oil
Juice of 1 lemon
1 teaspoon sea salt flakes

Beef liver is often overlooked by American cooks but deserves a place in the kitchen—and not only because it's high in iron and zinc, important nutrients that support the immune system. It's also delicious, especially when marinated for a few hours in buttermilk to temper the slight bitterness of the liver. Serve this dish with winter fava (page 65; omit the siglino in the topping), which is a cinch to whip up while the liver is marinating.

1. Lay a couple of thyme and oregano sprigs in a glass container, pour some buttermilk over them, then add the liver and a couple more sprigs from each herb. Pour in the remaining buttermilk to completely submerge the liver. Cover the container and put it in the fridge for at least 4 and up to 8 hours.

2. In a deep dish or a narrow tray, combine the remaining herb sprigs, the pepper, and olive oil. Cover and let stand on the counter and infuse while the liver is marinating.

3. Preheat your grill to medium-high. Remove the liver from the container, discard the marinade, and dry the liver very well with paper towels.

4. Coat the liver with some of the infused olive oil. Place on the grill about 4 inches (10 cm) above the fire. Grill until browned, about 3 minutes per side, turning once. Do not overcook; it should still be pink inside.

5. Put it on a serving plate, pour the rest of the infused olive oil over it, drizzle with the lemon juice, season with salt, and serve garnished with the herbs from the olive oil.

"OF THE HOUR"

On Greek restaurant menus you'll often find two main-dish categories: "Cooked" (Μαγειρευτά) and, roughly translated, "Of the Hour" (Ψητά της ώρας). The first refers to home-style dishes that are made in larger quantities in advance—like moussaka, pastitsio, meatballs, roast lamb like the Lamb Slow-Cooked in the Gastra (page 225), and so on. The second refers to dishes that are made to order—grilled seafood and souvlaki, steaks, fried squid, that kind of thing. As Kardamili has become more popular with out-of-towners, the owner of one of the busier restaurants in the village decided to close altogether for a few weeks during the height of the summer vacation season. The reason? Tablefuls of tourists ordering only "of the hour" dishes and jamming up the kitchen.

papou's meat sauce

Serves 4

¼ cup (60 ml) extra-virgin olive oil
½ teaspoon freshly ground black
    pepper, plus more to taste
1 pound (455 g) ground beef (see
    Note)
2 cloves garlic, minced
2 medium onions, chopped
2 teaspoons sea salt flakes, plus
    more to taste
1 teaspoon ground cumin
2 large carrots, peeled and
    chopped in a food processor
    or as finely as possible with
    a knife
1 (12-ounce/330-ml) bottle beer
1 (6-ounce/170-g) can tomato
    paste
1 (14-ounce/420-ml) can crushed
    tomatoes
1 (8-ounce/240-ml) can V8 juice
2 teaspoons dried oregano
Handful of fresh parsley, chopped
Grated parmesan cheese, for
    serving

Serve this sauce over pasta, topped with parmesan cheese and a little fresh parsley.

1. Heat the olive oil in a large saucepan over high heat. Add the pepper and lower the heat to medium-high. Add the beef and cook, stirring with a wooden spoon, until the meat is browned and no liquid remains in the saucepan. Stir in the garlic and cook until fragrant, about 2 minutes.

2. Add the onions, sprinkle 2 teaspoons salt over them, and let cook undisturbed for 30 seconds. Add the cumin. Mix well and continue to stir until the onions become translucent, 1 minute or so. Sauté until all the excess liquid in the pan has evaporated, about 5 minutes.

3. Add the carrots and any additional vegetables, if using (see Note; any extra vegetables may require additional cooking time and more salt), and stir. If the ingredients start to stick to the bottom of the pan, pour in a splash of the beer. Cook for 4 to 5 minutes and continue to add beer as needed.

4. Mix in the tomato paste, stir well for 1 minute, then add the remaining beer, the crushed tomatoes, and V8 juice to the sauce and stir. Bring to a boil, then turn the heat to low. Simmer for 30 minutes, stirring occasionally.

5. Taste for salt and pepper and add more if needed. Cook for another 20 to 30 minutes. Add the oregano and parsley and cook for an additional 1 to 2 minutes. (The oregano and parsley should be added just minutes before the sauce is ready.) The sauce is ready when you can drag the spoon along the bottom of the pan and there is no excess liquid and the sauce is slow to close the gap. Serve hot with more parsley and grated parmesan cheese.

NOTE: You can halve the ground beef and replace the rest with finely chopped eggplant or zucchini. This is great to do when these vegetables are in season for a flavorful twist.

beef stew with carrots and potatoes

Serves 6

¼ cup (60 ml) extra-virgin olive oil
Sea salt flakes and freshly ground
  black pepper
2 pounds (910 g) beef stew meat
  (cubed chuck roast)
2 medium onions, diced
3 cloves garlic, minced
1 tablespoon tomato paste
6 cups (1.4 L) beef stock
1 bay leaf
4 carrots, peeled and diced
1 pound (455 g) potatoes, peeled
  and cubed
2 cups (290 g) fresh or frozen peas,
  or 1 (15-ounce/425-g) can,
  drained
2 tablespoons minced fresh
  parsley

This is our version of the classic wintry beef stew, which we sometimes cook in the oven in a gastra. A drizzle of honey when you add the broth is an unusual but welcome addition if you'd like to try that.

1. Heat a large stockpot over medium-high heat and add the olive oil. Salt and pepper all sides of the cubed beef and then add half of it to the pot in a single layer. Brown on all sides, then remove from the pot and set aside on a plate. Repeat with the remaining meat.

2. Add the onions and garlic to the pot and cook until the onions begin to soften, about 2 minutes. Add the tomato paste, mix all together, and cook for another 2 minutes.

3. Pour in the stock and stir well. Return the beef with all of its juices back to the pot. Season with more salt and pepper. Add the bay leaf. Bring to a boil, then reduce the heat to low, cover your pot, and simmer for 1½ to 2 hours.

4. Add the carrots and potatoes. Cover and simmer until the carrots and potatoes are just tender, 30 to 45 minutes. For the last 10 minutes, add the peas and let them simmer. Remove the bay leaf and stir in the parsley. Serve.

lamb fricassee with dill, lemon, and lettuce

Serves 6 to 8

¾ cup (180 ml) extra-virgin olive oil
½ teaspoon freshly ground black
    pepper, plus more if needed
4 pounds (1.8 kg) lamb shoulder,
    cut into pieces
4 cloves garlic, chopped
8 to 10 scallions, chopped (white
    parts ½ inch/12 mm thick,
    green parts 1 inch/2.5 cm
    thick)
3 teaspoons sea salt flakes, plus
    more to taste
3 large heads of lettuce
½ cup (25 g) chopped fresh dill
2 large eggs
Juice of 2 lemons

This dish of rich braised lamb and lettuce is enriched with a lemony egg sauce that becomes almost creamy as it's warmed in the pot.

1. Heat the olive oil in a large pot over high heat. Add the pepper and lower the heat to medium-high. Add the lamb and cook, stirring with a wooden spoon, until the meat is browned. Stir in the garlic and cook until fragrant, about 2 minutes.

2. Add the scallions, sprinkle 2 teaspoons salt over them, and add 2 cups (480 ml) water. Lower the heat to medium and bring to a boil.

3. Chop the lettuce into 2-inch (5-cm) pieces.

4. When the water in the pot has almost evaporated, add the lettuce, dill, and another 1 teaspoon salt; lower the heat to medium-low, cover, and simmer until there is about 1½ cups (360 ml) of liquid left in the pot.

5. In a bowl, beat the eggs. Add the lemon juice and mix well. Slowly and while stirring, add about 1 cup (240 ml) of the liquid from the pot to the eggs, 1 tablespoon at a time, until the bowl is hot to the touch.

6. Add the egg-lemon mixture to the pot, mix well, and serve immediately.

lamb slow-cooked in the gastra

Serves 4

5 sprigs fresh rosemary
3 sprigs fresh thyme
3 sprigs fresh oregano
3 sprigs fresh sage
2 teaspoons sea salt flakes
2 teaspoons freshly ground black
    pepper
1 cup (240 ml) white wine
1 (2 to 3 pound/910 g to 1.4 kg) leg
    of lamb, cut into three or four
    pieces to fit in your gastra
½ cup (120 ml) extra-virgin olive oil
1 head of garlic, washed but
    unpeeled, cut in half
    horizontally
2 bay leaves
½ cup (120 ml) warm water,
    if needed
Juice of 2 lemons

This hearty, tender lamb, redolent with fresh herbs, is wonderful with Crispy Roasted Potatoes (page 127; shown opposite), or mashed or baked potatoes.

1. Take the leaves from one sprig of each fresh herb, finely chop them, and mix with the salt and pepper. Set aside.

2. Lay the remaining 4 sprigs rosemary in the bottom of a gastra and pour the wine over them.

3. Rub each piece of lamb with some of the olive oil, then with the herb mixture. Lay the lamb pieces on top of the rosemary. Arrange the remaining herb sprigs, the two garlic halves, and bay leaves in between the lamb pieces.

4. Pour the remaining olive oil over the two garlic halves, cover the gastra, and put it in a cold oven. Turn the oven on to 400°F (205°C). Bake for 40 minutes, then lower the heat to 350°F (175°C) and bake for 2 hours longer.

5. Take the gastra out of the oven and turn the lamb pieces over. If all the liquid has evaporated, add the warm water. (If there is liquid in the pot, no need to add more.) Return the gastra to the oven without the lid and bake for 20 to 25 minutes, until nicely browned.

6. Put the lamb on a serving platter. Remove and discard the herb sprigs and bay leaves.

7. Into a small bowl, squeeze the garlic cloves out of the skins, add the remaining juices from the gastra and the lemon juice, and whisk all together. Pour over the lamb and serve.

roasted pork tenderloin in honey, orange, and red wine vinegar glaze

Serves 4

1 pound (455 g) boneless pork
    tenderloin
¼ cup (60 ml) extra-virgin olive oil
¼ cup (60 ml) freshly squeezed
    orange juice
¼ cup (60 ml) red wine vinegar
½ cup (120 ml) honey
2 teaspoons sea salt flakes
1 teaspoon finely chopped fresh
    thyme, plus more for garnish
1 teaspoon finely chopped fresh
    rosemary, plus more for
    garnish
1½ teaspoons finely chopped fresh
    ginger
3 cloves garlic, minced
1 medium onion, finely chopped
1 teaspoon freshly ground black
    pepper

Marinating and basting with a flavorful sweet-sour sauce keeps lean pork tenderloin from drying out in the oven.

1. Pierce the tenderloin all over with a fork. In a bowl, combine the pork with the olive oil, orange juice, vinegar, honey, salt, thyme, rosemary, ginger, garlic, and onion, cover, and put in the refrigerator to marinate for at least 2 hours, or up to a day.

2. Preheat the oven to 400°F (205°C).

3. Put the pork in a glass baking dish and pour the marinade over the top. Sprinkle on the black pepper. Roast for 25 to 35 minutes, until the internal temperature of the pork reaches 150°F (65°C). During the cooking process, baste the pork with the marinade two or three times.

4. Remove from the oven, transfer the pork to a carving board to rest for at least 5 minutes, and pour the juices from the baking dish into a small saucepan. Bring to a simmer over medium heat and cook until reduced by half.

5. Slice the pork crosswise into slices that are 1½ inch (4 cm) thick. Transfer to a serving platter and pour the reduced cooking juices over the top. Garnish with fresh thyme and rosemary and serve.

roast rabbit with garden herbs and potatoes

Serves 4

½ cup (120 ml) extra-virgin olive oil
1 (2 to 2½ pound/about 1 kg)
    whole rabbit
3 sprigs fresh lavender
3 sprigs fresh rosemary
3 sprigs fresh marjoram
3 sprigs fresh oregano
2 sprigs fresh sage
5 sprigs fresh thyme
1 medium onion, sliced
1 teaspoon sea salt flakes
1 teaspoon freshly ground black
    pepper
3 to 4 potatoes, cut into 1 × 2-inch
    (2.5 × 5-cm) pieces

Farmed rabbit meat tastes, well, a lot like chicken, but it's leaner—and because rabbits can be raised without grain-based food they are considered relatively sustainable. We get our rabbit from friends or from the butcher. It is a popular meat in Greece and commonly found on restaurant menus. With tons of fresh herbs, and surrounded by chunks of roasted potatoes, this rabbit is a fine introduction if you haven't cooked it before.

1. Preheat the oven to 350°F (175°C). Coat the bottom of a roasting pan with ¼ cup (60 ml) of the olive oil.

2. Place the rabbit in the center of the roasting pan and stuff with 2 sprigs lavender, 2 sprigs rosemary, 2 sprigs marjoram, 2 sprigs oregano, 2 sprigs sage, and 4 sprigs thyme, followed by one-quarter of the sliced onion.

3. Season the rabbit outside and inside with ½ teaspoon each of salt and pepper.

4. Place the potatoes and remaining onion slices around the rabbit and sprinkle the rest of the salt and pepper on them. Chop the remaining sprigs of herbs and place them around the rabbit and in the bed of potatoes and onion. Drizzle the remaining ¼ cup (60 ml) olive oil on top of the rabbit and potatoes.

5. Bake for 1 hour 15 minutes, basting periodically. If the rabbit starts to look too crisp or brown, cover it with aluminum foil.

6. Remove from the oven and let the rabbit rest for 15 minutes before carving. This will help retain all the juices. Serve with the potatoes and onion.

CHAPTER SEVEN

Sundries

Baked
Goods,
Sweets,
and Drinks

Αγάλι-αγάλι γίνεται
η αγουρίδα μέλι.

Slowly, slowly the
sour grape becomes
honey.

THANK GOD FOR TSIKOUDIA

Nicholas: When I was younger and slightly more adventurous (and quite a bit less prudent) than I am now, a buddy and I set sail in a thirty-foot boat from Crete to Kythira—it'd be about a ten-hour trip. Some time after we left port, we made the horrific discovery that whoever had filled our water tanks—one for potable water and one for washing water—had mixed them up, so we had no clean drinking water.

After hours at sea, we were hungry and also a bit thirsty, so we dipped paximathia—these are the same dry rusks we use for dakos—into the seawater and ate them (this is *not recommended*, by the way), then washed it all down with copious amounts of high-proof tsikoudia. We survived—and thank God for tsikoudia.

Olivia: Was that the time you got lost?

Nicholas: It was, oddly enough. But the story of how the lights that looked from a distance to be the village where we were headed started to move as we neared them, and how we thought they were Italian fishing boats but they turned out to be the Russian fleet, is perhaps best saved for a different kind of book.

cretan paximathia (barley rusks)

Makes 16 rusks

About 4 cups (960 ml) warm water,
    110 to 115°F (43 to 46°C)
50 grams fresh yeast, or
    2 tablespoons active dry yeast,
    or 5 teaspoons instant yeast
2 tablespoons all-purpose flour,
    plus more for dusting
½ teaspoon honey
7 cups (1 kg) whole barley flour
3 cups (375 g) whole wheat flour
1½ teaspoons sea salt flakes
1 cup (240 ml) extra-virgin olive oil

These are the rusks used to make the dakos on pages 38 and 40.

1. In a measuring cup, put 1½ cups (360 ml) of the warm water, add the yeast and the all-purpose flour, and mix well. Set aside to dissolve the yeast.

2. In another cup, combine 1 cup (240 ml) of the warm water and the honey and stir to dissolve.

3. In a large wooden bowl, whisk together the whole barley and whole wheat flours and the salt, make a well in the center, and pour in the water with the yeast, the water with the honey, and the olive oil. Gradually mix the flours into the liquids with a wooden spoon.

4. Before you start kneading, warm your hands by running them under warm water, clapping them dry, and rubbing them together. Knead for about 15 minutes, adding more warm water slowly until the dough is no longer flaky or dry; you do not have to use all the water, just as much as it will take so the dough does not stick to the walls of the bowl.

5. Cover the bowl with a damp kitchen towel and let rest in a warm place for 45 minutes.

6. Punch down the dough and knead again. The harder you knead, the fluffier the rusks are going to be.

7. Divide the dough into four pieces and then divide each piece again into four pieces to make sixteen pieces.

8. Shape each piece into a ball and either flatten it or roll it into a cylinder and then shape it into a small donut. With a sharp knife, make a horizontal cut almost all the way through, place on a baking sheet, keep covered with a damp kitchen towel, and let them rise again to almost double their size.

9. Preheat the oven to 350°F (175°C).

10. Uncover the baking sheet and place it in the oven and bake for 1 hour, then remove from the oven and let cool for a bit. Once they are cool enough to handle, separate the tops from the bottoms, where you made the cut before baking. Return, cut side up, to the baking sheet.

11. Lower the oven temperature to 210°F (100°C) and bake again for another 60 to 90 minutes, until the rusks are hard. Let cool, covered with a *dry* towel, for several hours or overnight.

12. Store in an airtight container in a cool, dark place. They will be good for 1 to 2 months. Do not refrigerate.

BAR MUFFINS

Chloe: Down a narrow street cobbled with smooth round stones just steps from Kardamili's beach is one of the world's great bars (in our opinion): 1866 Beer Bar, or just "the jazz bar," as Dad refers to it. It's where we often go for drinks after dinner, the place where we can be sure to run into someone we know, where we catch up on town news and gossip.

Nicholas: It's where I go every night to get my muffins.

Chloe: Oddly enough, this is true. Dad will head over to the bar at night to pick up a muffin—the chocolate ones are the best—to have for breakfast the next morning. Of course, he'll usually stay and have a bottle of his favorite beer, Fix, and engage in multiple lengthy conversations as well—it sometimes seems as if he knows everyone in town, and they always have something to talk about.

The bar has a laid-back vibe that spills outside to the little tables set up in front of the thick-walled stone building in the late evenings. The kitchen serves classic comfort foods (including a burger and fries that any good New York City tavern would be proud to offer), and the bar features a rotating selection of local beers on tap—and a bartender who knows his way around a mojito and will make even out-of-towners ordering ouzo shots feel at home (though he might raise a subtle eyebrow in their direction; tsipouro is the drink of choice among locals; see the Rakokazano, page 257). The bar is the hub of the annual Kardamili Jazz Festival in spring, and where the musicians gather for impromptu jam sessions after their scheduled shows at other venues—it's definitely the place to be after hours. And just this year, the owner added a breakfast menu and opened a lovely garden area in the back, shaded by loquat (moúsmoulo), citrus, and fig trees.

So, theoretically, Dad could get his morning muffin there *in the morning*.

bread baked
in the gastra

Makes 1 loaf

1½ cups (360 ml) warm water,
     110 to 115°F (43 to 46°C)
1 teaspoon active dry yeast
3 cups (375 g) all-purpose flour,
     plus more for dusting
1½ teaspoons sea salt flakes, finely
     ground
2 tablespoons coarse semolina
1 large egg
2 tablespoons sesame or poppy
     seeds

Not only is the gastra the ideal cooking vessel for stews and long-cooked braised dishes, it's also commonly used like a cloche bread baker. The clay pot traps steam from the baking dough inside, which results in a crackly-crisp crust.

It's important that your water is the right temperature—too hot and it'll kill the yeast and your bread won't rise; too cold and it'll take forever to proof.

1. In a measuring cup, combine the warm water with the yeast and let it stand in a warm place for 10 to 20 minutes; you will have a light brown liquid with small bubbles on the top.

2. In a large bowl, whisk together the flour and salt. Add the yeast water to the flour. Using a wooden spoon, stir until a shaggy dough forms; it will be wet and very sticky to the touch. Cover the bowl with a damp kitchen towel or plastic wrap and let the dough rest and rise in a warm place for 15 to 20 minutes.

3. Poke the dough with your finger and, using your hand or a rubber spatula, start scraping the dough from the edges of the bowl toward the center to work the dough loose from the sides and fold it into the center of the bowl. Turn the bowl on its side, and repeat until all the dough has been pulled from the sides and folded into the center. Cover again and let the dough rest and rise for another 1 to 1½ hours.

4. Generously flour a spot on your counter, transfer the dough to the floured counter, and with floured hands quickly shape it into a ball.

5. Put the gastra with its lid on in the cold oven and turn the oven to 450°F (230°C).

6. Meanwhile, sprinkle the semolina on a sheet of parchment paper, transfer the dough onto it, and fold the edges of the paper; cover the dough again with a damp kitchen towel, and let it rest for 30 minutes.

7. In a small bowl, beat the egg.

8. Using oven mitts, and having a place ready to set the hot gastra, remove the gastra from the oven and take off the lid. Uncover the dough and carefully transfer the dough, on the parchment paper, to the gastra, holding the parchment paper by its edges. Quickly brush the top of the dough with the egg and sprinkle with sesame or poppy seeds. Cover the gastra and return it to the oven. Bake for 40 minutes, then remove the lid and bake for 15 minutes more.

9. Remove the bread from the gastra, place on a wire rack without the parchment paper, and let cool for 10 minutes before slicing.

zucchini and olive oil bread

Makes one 9 × 5-inch
(23 × 12-cm) loaf

⅓ cup (80 ml) extra-virgin olive oil,
  plus more for the pan
2 cups (250 g) all-purpose flour
1 teaspoon baking powder
1 teaspoon baking soda
1 teaspoon sea salt flakes
1 teaspoon ground cinnamon
½ cup (120 ml) honey
1 large egg
½ cup (120 ml) whole milk Greek
  yogurt
1½ teaspoons vanilla extract
1 cup (110 g) shredded zucchini
  (about 1 large)
1 teaspoon grated orange zest
½ cup (85 g) dark chocolate
  chunks (optional)
½ cup (60 g) chopped walnuts
  (optional)

We love lightly sweetened quick breads like this one, which requires only a couple bowls and a whisk—no mixer necessary. Add walnuts and dark chocolate chunks for a more dessert-like bread.

1. Preheat the oven to 350°F (175°C). Oil a 9 × 5-inch (23 × 12-cm) loaf pan.

2. In a large bowl, whisk the flour, baking powder, baking soda, salt, and cinnamon together. Set aside.

3. In a medium bowl, whisk the olive oil, honey, egg, yogurt, and vanilla together until combined.

4. Pour the wet ingredients into the dry ingredients and mix with a large wooden spoon or rubber spatula until combined. Fold in the zucchini, orange zest, and chocolate chunks (if using).

5. Spread the batter in the prepared pan and top with the walnuts (if using). Bake for 40 to 50 minutes, until a toothpick inserted in the center comes out clean. If you find the top of the bread is browning too quickly, loosely cover it with aluminum foil.

6. Remove from the oven and set on a wire rack to cool. Allow to cool completely before slicing and serving.

carrot cake with honey

Makes one 13 × 9-inch
(33 × 23-cm) cake

Packed with carrots, fragrant with cool-weather spices, and perfectly moist due to the olive oil and honey, this cake is sure to become a favorite—and it's easy to throw together. The topping of crumbled fresh cheese, good honey, and a light sprinkle of walnuts is a delicious alternative to sugary frosting.

FOR THE CAKE

1 cup (240 ml) extra-virgin olive oil, plus more for the pan

2¼ cups (280 g) all-purpose flour, plus more for the pan

2 teaspoons baking powder

1 teaspoon baking soda

1 teaspoon sea salt flakes

2½ teaspoons ground cinnamon

¾ teaspoon grated nutmeg

3 large eggs

½ cup (120 ml) honey

½ cup (120 ml) whole milk Greek yogurt

1 tablespoon vanilla extract

3 cups (330 g) grated carrots

FOR THE TOPPING

1 cup (245 g) crumbled fresh mizithra cheese (or ricotta)

2 to 4 tablespoons honey

¼ cup (30 g) chopped walnuts

1. Make the cake: Preheat the oven to 350°F (175°C). Oil and flour a 13 × 9-inch (33 × 23-cm) baking pan (you can also use a ring mold pan).

2. In a large bowl, whisk together the flour, baking powder, baking soda, salt, cinnamon, and nutmeg.

3. In a separate large bowl, beat the eggs, olive oil, honey, yogurt, and vanilla until combined. Add the dry ingredients to the wet ingredients and fully mix together, then stir in the carrots. Pour the batter into the prepared baking pan.

4. Bake for 25 to 35 minutes, until a toothpick inserted in the center comes out clean. Remove from the oven and set on a wire rack to cool. Allow to cool completely.

5. Top with crumbles of cheese, a drizzle of honey, and a sprinkle of walnuts, then slice and serve.

melomakarona

Makes 50 to 60 cookies

FOR THE SYRUP

3 cinnamon sticks

3 to 4 whole cloves

1 orange, cut into quarters

3 cups (720 ml) honey

FOR THE COOKIES

7¼ cups (905 g) all-purpose flour

1 cup (180 g) fine semolina flour

1¾ cups (420 ml) orange juice

2¼ cups (300 ml) extra-virgin
    olive oil

¼ cup (60 ml) honey

½ teaspoon ground cloves

1 tablespoon ground cinnamon

¼ teaspoon grated nutmeg

Grated zest of 2 oranges

1 cup (120 g) crushed walnuts

These orange-scented cookies, softened in a honey syrup infused with whole spices, are traditionally made at Christmas. NOTE: The syrup must be made at least 5 hours in advance so it is completely cool when the cookies are submerged in it.

1. Put 1¾ cups (420 ml) water, the cinnamon, cloves, and orange into a pot and bring to a boil. As soon as it boils, remove from the heat and let stand for 10 minutes.

2. Add the honey and stir until all the honey is dissolved.

3. Let the syrup cool completely. The cinnamon and cloves can stay in the syrup; remove the orange pieces.

4. Make the cookies: Preheat the oven to 350°F (175°C). Line baking sheets with parchment paper.

5. Sift together the flour and semolina and set aside.

6. In a large bowl, combine all the remaining ingredients except the walnuts and mix well. Fold in the flour mixture; do not overmix or it will separate. Mold the dough into ovals 1½ to 2 inches (4 to 5 cm) in length, trying to keep them as equally sized as possible. Place on the prepared baking sheets and bake for 20 to 25 minutes, until crunchy and dark golden brown.

7. Immediately after removing from the oven, submerge the cookies in the cooled syrup for 15 seconds. Remove from the syrup, place on a plate, and sprinkle the crushed walnuts on top. If you'd like, drizzle additional syrup on top. They keep for up to 1 week stored in an airtight container.

sea salt and honey chocolate chunk cookies

Makes 16 to 20 cookies

¼ cup (60 ml) extra-virgin olive oil
¼ cup (60 ml) tahini
½ cup (120 ml) honey
1 tablespoon vanilla extract
2 large eggs
2¼ cups (180 g) all-purpose flour
1 teaspoon baking soda
½ teaspoon finely ground sea salt
    flakes
1 teaspoon ground cinnamon
¼ cup (40 g) sesame seeds
1½ cups (255 g) dark chocolate
    chunks
Sea salt flakes for topping
    (optional)

Chocolate chunk cookies with no butter or sugar? It took us a while to come up with the perfect proportions of olive oil, tahini, and honey, but these cookies were worth the trial and error.

1. In a large bowl, combine the olive oil, tahini, honey, and vanilla. Add the eggs and mix until thoroughly combined.

2. In a separate bowl, whisk together the flour, baking soda, salt, cinnamon, and sesame seeds. Add the dry ingredients to the wet ingredients and gently mix until just combined; don't overmix. Fold in the chocolate chunks with a rubber spatula. Put the dough in a covered container and into the refrigerator to chill for at least 2 hours, or up to 2 days.

3. When ready to bake, preheat the oven to 375°F (190°C). Line baking sheets with parchment paper.

4. Scoop the dough into 16 to 20 balls and press flat. Place on the baking sheet at least 3 inches (7.5 cm) apart. Bake for 10 to 12 minutes. Sprinkle the cookies with sea salt flakes (if using) when they come out of the oven. Let cool for at least 20 minutes on the baking sheets, then transfer to a plate or store in an airtight container for 3 days or freeze for up to 3 months.

fig frozen yogurt

Serves 8 to 10

2¼ pounds (1 L) whole milk Greek yogurt
9 ounces (255 g) figs, stemmed and quartered
5 tablespoons honey

This treat could not be simpler. The frozen yogurt is delicious plain straight from the freezer container, but try it topped with crushed walnuts and a drizzle of more honey or spoonful of homemade fig jam (page 251).

1. In a large bowl, combine all the ingredients in a stand mixer with the paddle attachment and mix on high speed for 15 minutes. Transfer to a freezer-safe container and freeze for about 4 hours, until firm.

2. Before serving, let the frozen yogurt stand at room temperature for 5 to 10 minutes to soften enough to scoop easily.

fresh honey-orange marmalade

Makes 1 (12½-ounce/370-ml) jar

1 organic orange
4 to 5 tablespoons honey

Marmalade doesn't have to involve hours of work and loads of sugar. This simple one, with just enough honey to offset the tartness of the fruit, can be whipped up at a moment's notice—no cooking needed.

1. Wash the orange thoroughly. Quarter it and remove any seeds. Place half of the orange pieces (with the peel still on) in a mini food processor. Add the honey, then place the remaining pieces of orange on top. Process until there are no more large chunks of orange. Store in a covered container in the refrigerator until ready to serve.

fig jam with honey

Makes about 4 half-pint (240-ml) jars

2¼ pounds (1 kg) fresh figs,
    stemmed and halved or
    quartered if large
Juice and grated zest of 1 lemon
Juice of 1 orange
About 1½ cups (455 g) honey
2 to 3 cinnamon sticks

We like to serve spoonfuls of this jam over fig frozen yogurt (page 248) for a double hit of fruit and honey.

1. Put the figs in a large pot and add the lemon and orange juice. Follow with the zest of the lemon. Let the ingredients sit for 30 minutes to let the figs soak up the flavors.

2. Bring to a boil over medium-high heat and boil for 2 to 3 minutes. Lower the heat and add the honey and cinnamon. Stir well so the honey begins to dissolve in the juices. Simmer for 40 minutes if canning, 50 minutes if not.

3. Store in a container in the refrigerator or can the jam for storage at room temperature: Sterilize the jars and heat the lids according to the jar manufacturer's instructions. If you are planning to keep your jam around for a lengthy amount of time, you should cook it in the pot for only 40 minutes and then another 10 in the jars. To can the jam, either sterilize the jars and heat the lids according to the jar manufacturer's instructions or put the half-pint glass canning jars with their lids (separated) in a large pot with water to cover and bring to a boil. Remove the jars from the water, drain them of water, set them upside down to dry on a towel. Make sure they are completely dry before you fill with jam, and fill each one with hot jam, leaving around ½ inch (12 mm) of space at the top. Screw on new lids finger-tight and place the jars in the pot of boiling water; return to a full boil and boil for 10 minutes. Transfer the jars to a folded towel, pat the tops dry, and let them cool for 12 hours; refrigerate any jars that don't seal. (For detailed canning instructions, see the National Center for Home Food Preservation website or a trusted canning book.)

feta wrapped in phyllo with sesame and honey

Serves 2 to 4

2 sheets phyllo dough
2 tablespoons extra-virgin olive oil,
    plus more for the top
4 ounces (115 g) feta cheese in a
    square block, cut in half
2 tablespoons honey
1 tablespoon white sesame seeds
1 teaspoon black sesame seeds

This is one of Chloe's absolute favorite Greek dishes to eat when visiting. The first time we ate it together was at a tiny taverna on the beach in Koufonisia, a Greek island where a friend of ours has a house. We have to order it every time we go there (which is just about daily when in Koufonisia)—and without fail, Chloe will burn her mouth because she can't wait to devour it before it cools off. This dish can be enjoyed at any point in a meal—as a starter, a shared meze, a side, or at the end of a meal with wine and fruit.

1. Preheat the oven to 350°F (175°C).

2. Brush a sheet of phyllo dough with half of the olive oil. Place the feta halves next to each other at the bottom of the sheet to form a rectangle. Fold the phyllo dough over the sides of the cheese, then roll the cheese in the phyllo until you've reached the end of the sheet. Brush the other phyllo sheet with the remaining olive oil and rewrap the packet, ensuring there are no holes in your phyllo layer.

3. Place the cheese packet in a baking dish and brush the top with additional olive oil. Bake for 20 minutes, or until the dough is lightly browned.

4. Remove from the oven and transfer to a serving plate. Drizzle with the honey and sprinkle the top with sesame seeds. Attempt to let it cool before consuming so you don't burn your mouth.

blueberry pastries with lemon yogurt frosting

Makes 3

FOR THE PASTRIES

2 cups (290 g) fresh blueberries

½ cup (120 ml) honey

2 tablespoons fresh lemon juice

1 (17.25-ounce/490-g) package frozen puff pastry or Greek equivalent, thawed

1 large egg, beaten

FOR THE FROSTING AND TOPPING

½ cup (120 ml) whole milk Greek yogurt

2 tablespoons honey

1 to 2 tablespoons fresh lemon juice

1 teaspoon vanilla extract

1 to 2 teaspoons crushed freeze-dried blueberries

1 teaspoon chopped fresh mint

One of the American snacks we missed while in Greece were blueberry toaster pastries, so we decided to create our own version with what we had available—and to our delight ours was even better than the packaged pastry we had craved.

1. Make the pastries: In a small saucepan over medium heat, combine the blueberries, honey, and lemon juice. Use the back of a wooden spoon to crush the blueberries and then bring the mixture to a boil. Cook, stirring occasionally, until thickened, 15 to 20 minutes. Remove from the heat and let cool completely.

2. Preheat the oven to 350°F (175°C). Line a baking sheet with parchment paper.

3. Cut the puff pastry sheet into six equal squares. On three of the squares, brush beaten egg on the outside edges of the square and spoon blueberry filling throughout the middle. Top each square with the remaining pieces of pastry. Press the edges together and then seal with a fork. Transfer to the baking sheet and brush the tops with beaten egg. Bake for 15 to 20 minutes, until the pastry browns and puffs up.

4. Make the frosting and topping: Whisk the yogurt, honey, lemon juice, and vanilla together in a small bowl. Drizzle over the pastries and top with the freeze-dried blueberries and fresh mint. Serve.

THE RAKOKAZANO

When most people think of Greek liqueurs and liquors, they think of ouzo, but in fact, most people here don't drink ouzo—it's for the tourists (and, well, Gregory, Dimitri's cousin from Montreal). Greeks instead drink tsipouro ("CHIP-oo-roh," also called raki, depending on where in Greece you are). While ouzo is made from sugar fermented with commercial ethanol distilled with anise and heavily sweetened to disguise the ethanol flavor, tsipouro is lightly fermented from sweet, low-acidity fruits, predominantly grapes, and then distilled (in some areas with anise), and it contains no sweetener.

Our favorite variety is tsikoudia, which is made only in Crete and only from grapes. We get a supply in Crete once a year and bring it home, where we gather with friends and have our own rakokazano (raki-making party), distilling it a second time in a hand-crafted copper still out on the patio, for a smoother finish. We leave half of it as is and put the rest in small oak barrels to age for one to three months. This allows the tsikoudia to take on characteristics from the wood, turning it a caramel color with tasting notes of oak and vanilla.

yiayia's strawberry afternoon delight

Serves 2

2 cups (300 g) strawberries, halved
1 tablespoon honey
½ cup (120 ml) rakomelo or cognac
    (if you're using cognac, add an
    extra teaspoon of honey)
1 tablespoon fresh lemon juice
12 fresh mint leaves

We used to visit my yiayia in the same house that Dad grew up in, in Athens. Chloe and I loved when she made us υποβρύχιο, or "submarine," a spoonful of mastic, resin "teardrops" submerged in a glass of ice-cold water to soften them. It had a refreshing piney-minty taste. We also devoured little whitebait fish we would eat like fries. She also served this strawberry dessert, with soothing mountain tea (page 262) that she'd bring out after siesta. We'd sit on her veranda, surrounded by flowers and vines. Her recipe uses rakomelo, a Cretan spirit used to help digestion and remedy ailments. It's widely available outside of Greece, but if you can't find it, cognac can be substituted. —OLIVIA

1. Place the strawberries in a dish large enough to make a layer of strawberries no more than two strawberry halves deep.

2. In a bowl, thoroughly mix the honey, rakomelo, and lemon juice and pour over the strawberries.

3. Make sure all the strawberries are completely covered and coated on all sides, then place in the fridge and chill for 2 to 3 hours.

4. Garnish with the mint, serve, and enjoy with iced mountain tea.

mint and honey lemonade

Makes 4 cups (960 ml)

2 tablespoons honey
2 tablespoons boiling water
3 cups (720 ml) cold water
1 cup (240 ml) fresh lemon juice
8 fresh mint leaves, plus more for
    serving
Lemon slices

This cold drink not only is a symphony of flavors and aromas, but it's full of vitamins and antioxidants. Sweet and tart combine to make this delicious and refreshing summer beverage a new favorite.

1. In a liquid measuring cup, dissolve the honey in the boiling water.
2. In a 4-cup (960-ml) pitcher or bottle, combine the 3 cups (720 ml) cold water and the lemon juice. Add the honey-water mixture and then the mint. Mix well.
3. Serve with fresh mint leaves and a slice of lemon in each glass.

cleanse and soothe tea blend

Makes as much as you want

3 parts dried mountain tea (sideritis)
2 parts dried melissa
1 part dried purple heather
1 part dried verbena
1 part dried thistle

The exact amounts can vary depending on whether you're brewing a pot or cup of tea, but if you stick to this ratio as a guide it should taste delicious.

Dad always gave this tea to Chloe and me, telling us it was good for us and our digestion. When I did my own research into each herb's health benefits, my eyes grew wide: The tea boasts antioxidant and oxidative stress-reduction capabilities, and anti-inflammatory, anti-microbial, and gastro-protective properties, just to name a few. Like many herbs, these have been used for healing and remedies for thousands of years.

— OLIVIA

1. Remove the stalks and any bad leaves from the herbs.
2. Use a teapot with an infuser or cup infuser. Place all the herbs in the infuser.
3. Add boiling water and let steep for 10 minutes for a teapot and about 5 minutes for an individual cup.
4. Drink two cups for maximum relaxation.

FULL-MOON HERBS

According to local lore, the best time to gather wild herbs is just as they're blooming, when the days are sunny, and as soon after the night of the full moon as possible. The idea is to catch them when their essential oils are most plentiful, so they'll retain more flavor when they're dried. We have no idea why the full moon is important, but Greeks have been harvesting herbs this way for millennia, and all it takes is a glance at a lunar calendar and a little planning, so why wouldn't we try to do the same?

awake and revive tea blend

Makes as much as you want

3 parts dried mountain tea
    (sideritis)
2 parts dried peppermint
1 part dried nettles
1 part dried lemon verbena
Lemon or orange slices (optional)
Honey (optional)

The exact amounts can vary depending on whether you're brewing a pot or cup of tea, but if you stick to this ratio as a guide it should taste delicious.

1. Remove the stalks and any bad leaves from the herbs.
2. Use a teapot with an infuser or cup infuser. Place all the herbs in the infuser.
3. Add boiling water and let steep for 10 minutes for a teapot and about 5 minutes for an individual cup.
4. Add a slice of lemon or orange to your tea. If you prefer a sweeter brew, add honey to taste in your cup, starting with 1 teaspoon.

Index

Dedications

To David Perluck, my best friend, not to mention the biggest fan of my cooking. Your photography and artistry brought about a turning point in my life.

I remember when I asked you, "How come my photograph isn't as good as yours?" and you told me: "You have a camera. I have a camera. But along with a camera, I've also got something that took me more than thirty years to develop: an eye for the unique, the compelling, the almost inexplicable thing that makes an image or, more specifically, an image of an object, person, or place far more beautiful and desirable. Yes, you can make a picture, but I can communicate intangibles: quality, grace, value, and intelligence." So, this one time when you asked, "But we used the same ingredients, how come yours tastes so much better than mine?" I answered, "You have spices. I have spices. But along with the spices . . ." You are missed.

—Nicholas

To Uncle Craig: Though you passed when we were young, the memories we have of you—our own along with stories told to us from Mom and Mimi—are cherished. You were our best friend when we were young; we ate cereal with you every morning and loved going to the beach with you. Thank you for passing along your love of cooking and your joyful nature. We know you're watching over us both but wish you were still with us today. We hope this book makes you proud.

—Olivia and Chloe

Acknowledgments

Our fairy godmother, Lola Bubbosh, thank you. Without you, none of this would have been possible. Your inspiring imagination and infectious belief in us have taught us that with hard work and dedication, all our dreams can come true. Your spirit and never-wavering perseverance helped make *Sea Salt and Honey* a reality. Thank you, again, for always giving us the world.

Our photographer and stylist, Romas Foord and Polly Webb-Wilson, thank you for bringing our recipes to life more beautifully than we could have ever imagined. You both put us at ease by keeping us laughing throughout the shoot, and your constant encouragement made it possible for us to get it done. Even with the heat in the kitchen, you always kept cool. It was truly a joy to work with you and learn from your experience and elegance.

Our friends, Chiana Coronis and Solon Paissios, thank you for opening up your beautiful home, Villa Onor, and letting us take over your kitchen and the idyllic grounds to prepare and shoot some of our dishes there. You were always ready to lend a hand for chopping, stirring, or cleaning up, just like one of the family.

And finally, Liana Krissoff, Tricia Levi, Soyolmaa Lkhagvadorj, and the rest of the Harper Design team who helped create this book, thank you for your guidance and support through this process. We knew we were in the best of hands.

—Nicholas, Olivia, and Chloe

About the Authors

Nicholas Tsakiris, father of Olivia and Chloe, returned to his roots in Greece after decades in the United States. A prizewinning designer and architect, who is now a computer-networking engineer, he settled in an idyllic village, Kardamili, where he continues his tech work and his quest to live off the land.

Olivia followed soon after a brief stint at British *Vogue* and completing a master's degree in public relations. She now owns Salt Yoga in Kardamili, where she teaches classes by the seaside and also works for a local architecture firm. Now married and with a young son, she has settled happily into life there.

Chloe now calls New York City home, where she lives in Williamsburg, Brooklyn. When she's not working for Olo, the leading digital ordering solution for restaurants, she can be found teaching yoga or eating and creating content for foodstagrams: @food and @baking, and her own @sitdown.behungry. Chloe's obsession with recipes began at the start of her career when she worked with the director of product development at Hammond's Candies. She returns to Greece as often as possible, typically several times a year.

Nicholas, a lifelong experimenter with cooking and spices, inspired both his daughters to do the same. The recipes in *Sea Salt and Honey* are the result of years of family cooking and entertaining. Olivia and Nicholas both maintain large gardens, where they derive the bulk of their produce for cooking. Chloe is inspired by the myriad food shops and markets in NYC. All three pursue the spirit of Greek and Mediterranean life wherever they are.

seasaltnhoney.com
Instagram: @seasalt.n.honey